For the Culture!
For Detroit!
For Ky & DJ!
For My Ancestors!

CONTENTS

ILLUSTRATIONS

Figures

Tables

SERIES EDITORS' FOREWORD

If y'all actually believe that using "standard English" will dismantle white supremacy, then you not paying attention! If we, as teachers, truly believe that code-switching will dismantle white supremacy, we have a problem. If we honestly believe that code-switching will save Black people's lives, then we really ain't paying attention to what's happening in the world. Eric Garner was choked to death by a police officer while saying "I cannot breathe." Wouldn't you consider "I cannot breathe" "standard English" syntax?

(April Baker-Bell, Chapter 1)

Linguistic Justice is a book about Black people and identities, Black literacies and languages, and Black life and liberation. In fact, it is not only a book. It is also a complex love story about the valuable role teachers and teacher educators must play in supporting Black students to navigate and negotiate their linguistic, racial, and sociopolitical identities within multiple, hostile contexts. It is a love story about survival that is set against the realities of white supremacy that get materialized through racial injustices and linguistic violence. It is a love story against Anti-Blackness, generally, and against Anti-Black Linguistic Racism, specifically. And what a love story it is!

April Baker-Bell, a teacher-researcher-activist from Detroit, Michigan, describes how "traditional approaches to language education do not account for the emotional harm" that Black students painfully experience on a daily basis. Inside classrooms and throughout society, countless Black students are shamed for how they talk, walk, dress, breathe, think, live, and look. They are shamed for how they curiously ask questions, for how they creatively engage in solving problems, and for how they show up in classrooms and in the world. They are shamed because they are Black and they are doubly shamed if they are Black and speak Black Language. Thus, according to April, "If y'all actually believe that using 'standard English' will dismantle white supremacy, then you not paying attention!"

First, let's pay attention to *what* April teaches us and *how* she offers us an Antiracist Black Language Pedagogy as an approach that rejects the shaming of, and linguistic violence experienced by, Black people. She writes that this pedagogy is comprised of critical inquiry-based learning experiences that provide Black students with opportunities to learn about and use Black language as they simultaneously learn to reject Anti-Black Linguistic Racism. This approach also helps teachers and researchers come to terms with the many different ways Anti-Black Linguistic Racism gets dangerously normalized in our teaching and pedagogical engagements as well as in our research and advocacy efforts, which further degrades and shames Black students and their linguistic and racial identities.

Second, let's pay attention to *why* April teaches us about Antiracist Black Language Pedagogy. As an approach that confronts Anti-Black Linguistic Racism in the dispositions, stances, attitudes, and behaviors of teachers, teacher educators, and researchers, this pedagogy listens to, honors, and centers the voices, stories, and linguistic virtuosities of Black students. It not only raises awareness of Black linguistic consciousness (and April is not simply talking about "code-switching"!), but it seeks to dismantle Anti-Black Linguistic Racism. This dismantling must occur within classrooms and in our teaching of Black students, throughout society and in our daily interactions with Black people, and within our professional and research investments that purport to love Black lives. Thus, the *why* of this work, according to April, points to the reality that "If we, as teachers, truly believe that code-switching will dismantle white supremacy, we have a problem. If we honestly believe that code-switching will save Black people's lives, then we really ain't paying attention to what's happening in the world."

From the purposeful inclusion of the voices and counterstories of Black students to the composite character counterstories that demonstrate how Black students developed Black Linguistic Consciousness, April has written a brilliant book. From various images, dialogues, charts, graphs, instructional maps, artwork, stories, and weblinks to the curated learning experiences that represent Black Language Artifacts, April captures the beauty of Black Language and the significance of Antiracist Black Language Pedagogy. Within the pages of this book, or love story, she describes and documents the complexity, richness, and power of Black Language, of Black People, and of Black Linguistic Justice. This text, *Linguistic Justice: Black Language, Literacy, Identity, and Pedagogy,* deeply grounded in rigorous research and the highest levels of excellence, provides us with a much-needed direction in our ongoing efforts to reject the linguistic oppression of, and the racial violence directed toward, Black people.

Like the other books in our NCTE-Routledge Research Series, *Linguistic Justice* offers an important pedagogical innovation that focuses on the richness and beauty of the lives, literacies, and languages of Students of Color within and beyond P-12 literacy classrooms. The scope of books in our series includes an explicit focus on equity, justice, and antiracist literacy education; critical qualitative, quantitative, and mixed methodologies; a range of cutting-edge perspectives and approaches (e.g., sociocultural, cognitive, feminist, linguistic, pedagogical, critical, historical, anthropological); and research on the literacies of minoritized peoples as well as on diverse contexts (e.g., classrooms, school systems, families, communities) and forms of literacy (e.g., print, electronic, popular media). *Linguistic Justice* contributes to this scope by advocating *for* Antiracist Black Language Pedagogy and *against* anti-Blackness, racial violence, linguistic oppression, and white linguistic and cultural hegemony.

This is the book we've been dreaming of. We hope you are moved into action by April Baker-Bell's new book just as much as you are by the many other books in our series.

Valerie Kinloch
Renée and Richard Goldman Dean and Professor of
Education University of Pittsburgh
and
Susi Long
Professor of Early Childhood Education and Language and
Literacy University of South Carolina, Columbia

FOREWORD

At long last, this is the book we have all been waiting for. A book designed to develop our students' critical understanding of and historical consciousness about Black Language. A book that builds on that critical inquiry to motivate students to formulate ways of impacting and changing the linguistic status quo. As a leading member of a new generation of language and literacy scholar-teacher-activists, Dr. April Baker-Bell represents for Black Language and its speakers because she gets it. Props and much respect to Baker-Bell for her wisdom, her creative genius, and her years of teaching experience in the educational vineyard, which have given birth to the brilliantly crafted *Linguistic Justice: Black Language, Literacy, Identity, and Pedagogy.*

> If you white, you all right,
> If you brown, stick around,
> If you black, git back.
> —*From the Black Oral
> Tradition*

As an Elder who began her study and struggle in the throes of the mid-twentieth century Black Freedom Movement, and years later was baptized in the fire of "the linguistics of white supremacy" (Sledd, 1969), I had envisioned that such anti-Black messages would, by this twenty-first century, have been cast into the dustbin of history. Sadly, this has not been the case. As both Baker-Bell's research and present-day classroom experience with Black youth demonstrate, Black children continue to be "unconsciously trained to correlate blackness with wrongness and whiteness with rightness" (this volume, p. 24).

As long as anti-Black racism exists, anti-Black linguistic discrimination will continue to exist—despite more than a century of scholarship and research on Black Language (also referred to as African American Language, Black Dialect, African American Vernacular English, and "Negro English," the title of J.A. Harrison's article). Considered to be the first study of this linguistic phenomenon, Harrison's research was published in the journal *Anglia* in 1884. However, I use the labels "study" and "research" advisedly. While his description of "specimen Negroisms" (*sic*) suggests that he was aware of African language elements in the speech of slaves and their descendants, the Africanness was perceived to be inferior, pathological, deviant, and unnatural—e.g., he states that "much of the Negro's talk is baby-talk." Four decades later, in 1924 and 1925, English Language scholar George Krapp described the "English of the Negro" as "infantile English," his and Harrison's "baby-talk" description of Black Language corresponding to the racist assumption prevalent then (and now?) that Africans are lower forms of the human species whose evolution is incomplete.

By contrast, two Black scholars in Krapp's era, Drs. Carter G. Woodson and W. E.B. DuBois—neither a language scholar—referenced a scientific conception of "Negro English." DuBois, addressing the role and function of the "Negro University" in 1933, notes that a "Negro university…begins with Negroes [and] uses that variety of the English idiom which they understand." Woodson's admonition about "Negro dialect" is that Black youth should be "directed to study" the language." (See the full text of Woodson's advice in this volume, p. 24.)

In 1949, after nearly two decades of work, including years spent learning several West African languages at the University of London, Dr. Lorenzo Dow Turner (believed to be the first Black American linguist), published *Africanisms in the Gullah Dialect,* a descriptive study of the language of rural and urban Blacks in the coastal regions of South Carolina and Georgia, who were slave descendants of Africans from Nigeria, Liberia, Gambia, Sierra Leone, and other areas where West African language were and still are spoken. Turner found nearly 6,000 West African words in Gullah speech. Moreover, he accounted for Black folks' pronunciation and grammatical features in "Negro English" on scientific linguistic grounds, namely the influence of West African languages—indicating, for example, that "The English inter-dental fricative th does not exist in Gullah nor in the West African languages included in this study. In pronouncing English words containing this sound, both the Gullah speaker and the West African substitute [d] and [t], respectively, for the voiced and voiceless varieties of it."

With research grounded in linguistic science, rather than anti-Black racism and White supremacy, Turner's work revolutionized the field and paved the way for the explosion, in the 1960s, 1970s, and beyond, of research on "Negro Dialect"— these days commonly referred to as "African American Language," "Black Language," "African American English," or "U.S. Ebonics." Significantly, this research explosion includes the entry of Black scholars into the field—among them, Beryl Bailey, Arthur Spears, John Baugh, John Rickford, Marcylienna Morgan, the late Jerri Scott, Sonja Lanehart, Lisa Green, H. Samy Alim, and yours truly. My first presentation, "Black Power is Black Language," delivered in 1968 at a campus rally on Black Power; was published in 1972.

I love the United States of America. I love my country's flag. I love my country's language. I promise:

1. That I will not dishonor my country's speech by leaving off the last syllable of words.
2. That I will say a good American "yes" and "no" in place of an Indian grunt "um-hum" and "nup-um" or a foreign "ya" "yeh" or "nope."
3. That I will do my best to improve American speech by avoiding loud, rough tones, by enunciating distinctly, and by speaking pleasantly, clearly, and sincerely.
4. That I will learn to articulate correctly as many words as possible during the year.

("Better Speech Week" pledge, once cited regularly by
students throughout the Nation)

In 1917, the National Council of Teachers of English (NCTE), then in its organizational infancy, led a national promotion of "Better Speech Week." Gawthrop's "An Examination of the Attitudes of the NCTE Toward Language" (1965) notes that "this movement" was designed "to improve" student speech and that it "became something of a national phenomenon for the next ten or twelve years."

Over half a century after "Better Speech Week" swept the Nation, New York Public Schools Chancellor, late Dr. Richard Green, teamed up with then-Mayor Edward Koch, to focus on a list of twenty "speech demons." They were dedicated to eliminating these "demons possessing student tongues." A few examples from their list:

May I axe a question?
Hang the pitcher on the wall.
He be sick.
I ain't got none.
Where is the ball at?
The books is in the liberry.

In 1959, at Central High School in The D ("Detroit" in Black Talk), teacher-researcher Ruth Golden developed a language pedagogy grounded in the then-newly developed paradigm of contrastive analysis that was a part of the "linguistic method" for teaching a foreign language. She constructed sentences and phrases in Black and White Mainstream language patterns for oral drills in the classroom—for example, "John walks" (White Mainstream speech) vs. "John walk" (Black speech). One class of students, Golden's control group, were taught the abstract Latinate-based rules of English grammar, and the other class, the experimental group, were taught using oral pattern practice drills based on the linguistics of contrastive analysis. According to Golden, the experimental group significantly outperformed the control group in mastering the White Mainstream language patterns.

NCTE's "Better Speech Week," New York Public Schools' "speech demons" list, and Golden's elaborate contrastive analysis drills are examples of the language eradication paradigm, in which the goal is to eradicate speakers' native/home language patterns from their speech.

Beginning with the landmark *Brown v. Board* Supreme Court decision in 1954, the movement for Black integration into the White Mainstream gathered momentum, and significant resources and research funds were poured into language research and language education programs for Black students. Two things became increasingly clear. First, all the descriptive research on Black Language demonstrated that it was a highly developed, functional rule-governed linguistic system. Like other languages and dialects in the global world, Black speech was predictable and rule-governed. Second, the research indicated that Black students needed Black Language in order to communicate with other Black speakers in their families and communities. Thus, the language eradication philosophy and educational programs fell out of favor and were replaced with a philosophy and pedagogy of bi-dialectalism advocating that Black students needed to learn how to manipulate and speak both White and Black varieties of American English. In short, they needed to learn how to "code switch." However, this language policy presents a fundamental contradiction in language education for Black students. If African American Language (AAL) is systematic, rule-governed, and functional, as the voluminous research over several decades has established, then why is it continuing to be stigmatized and disrespected, even within the Black Language-speaking community itself (where you may hear it referred to as "breakin verbs" or "talkin ghetto"). Why can't this highly functional language be used in all situations? Why do Black Language speakers have to learn how to be bi-dialectal whereas White Mainstream English speakers can get along just fine—thank you, very much—being monodialectal? As I have signified in the past and now, "all languages are equal, but obviously some are more equal than others." And my boy, late White linguist, Dr. James Sledd, in a bold publication that sent shock waves throughout the language and educational communities, took promoters of bi-dia-lectalism to task and soundly condemned bi-dialectalism as the "linguistics of White supremacy" (1969). In sum, despite the voluminous studies of Black Language, spanning a century, and despite language scholars arguing the case for AAL, linguistic discrimination and linguistic injustice continue to prevail.

So what is the way forward? We need a language pedagogy that goes beyond defeatist slogans like, "that's just the way things are." This leads to stagnation, not change in the material and linguistic conditions of AAL speakers. We need a pedagogy which teaches us to explore why things are the way they are. A language pedagogy which forces us to confront the questions: How did the present social order come into being? What do we need to do to take it out of being? Teachers, language researchers, educational administrators, public policy theorists, critical race theorists, community activists, parents, high school youth—all need to be involved in the quest for linguistic justice, anti-racist pedagogy, and the disruption and destruction of anti-Black racism.

Enter Dr. April Baker-Bell with the book we have been waiting for. A ground-breaking twenty-first century book that sets a new standard for work on African American Language; that brings together theory, history, culture, activism in a multimodal, interactive teaching-learning curriculum undergirded by Anti-racist Black Language Pedagogy. The book's transformative lesson plans and inquiry-based teaching-learning experiences have been tested in the crucible of real world classrooms on both high school and college levels. A visionary work that advocates for collaboration with Latinx and other linguistically marginalized communities, that lays out an intellectually provocative teaching-research agenda that goes beyond outmoded paradigms of bi-dialectalism and code-switching, that creates a space for new knowledge, innovative pedagogical practices, and social justice activism, that provides us with ethnographic snapshots illustrating how Black students responded to the lessons as they learned about their own linguistic backgrounds and began to critically interrogate and resist White linguistic hegemony and anti-Black linguistic racism.

Mos def, this is the book we have been waiting for. That boldly confronts myths and misconceptions which continue to hold us back, such as competence in White Mainstream English can dismantle White supremacy. That takes us from sociolinguistic research to pedagogical practice to the ultimate goal of language liberation and linguistic justice.

In the book's bonus chapter, "THUG LIFE," Baker-Bell recounts her work in a classroom of college students who were enrolled in their university's pre-service teaching program. Her imaginative, innovative, intellectually stimulating multi-modal pedagogical strategies and techniques are on full display. Here we see a Master teacher at work, interacting with and probing the minds of her students as she disrupts old ways of thinking about language that have been ingrained in college students from Pre-K spaces throughout their educational journeys. As we witnessed in her work with high school students at Detroit's Leadership Academy, Baker-Bell is once again large and in charge, controlling the teaching-learning process as she pushes her students' minds to the limit.

Welcome to the lists of the language wars, Comrade Sista ABB!

Geneva Smitherman, Ph.D.
Professor Emerita of English
Core Faculty, African Studies Center
Affiliated Faculty, Language, Rhetoric and American Cultures
Michigan State University

References

Gawthrop, B. (1965). 1911–1929. In R.McDavid, Jr. (ed.), *An Examination of the Attitudes of the NCTE Toward Language* (pp. 7–15). Champaign/Urbana, IL: The National Council of Teachers of English.

Harrison, J. A. (1884). Negro English. *Anglia*, 7, 232–279.

Sledd, J. (1969). Bidialectalism: The linguistics of white supremacy. *English Journal*, 1307–1329.

Smitherman, G. (1968). Black Language is Black Power. Speech at Black Power Rally, 1968. Revised version published as Black Power is Black Language," in G. M. Simmons and H. D. Hutchinson (eds.) (1972). *Black Culture: Reading and Writing Black* (pp. 85–91). New York: Holt, Rinehart, Winston.

Turner, L. D. (1949). *Africanisms in the Gullah Dialect*. Chicago: University of Chicago Press.

ACKNOWLEDGMENTS

In the darkest and lightest moments, I've felt the presence of my creator and my ancestors reminding me that this journey is bigger than me. Ase!

To my babies, Ky and DJ: Knowing that you two have to live in this world has made me more courageous, fierce, determined, and intentional about my work. The best part of my journey writing this book was the two of you. Though I may not have appeared happy about your petty sibling quarrels throughout this process, I was always deeply appreciative of the distractions because they prevented me from being the perfectionist that we all know I can be. To Dominic Bell Sr.: Thank you for keeping me nurtured, nourished, and whole while writing this book! I appreciate you being the peace that calmed many of my hard days. I thank you for being patient, kind, flexible, and self-sacrificing! Thank you for supporting me and loving me deeply throughout this process!

I am grateful for the support that I have received from my family both near and far. To my parents and first teachers, Anthony Baker Sr. and Brenda Baker: Thank you for inspiring me, supporting me, and teaching me how to read, critique, and respond to the world. Thanks for the strength, courage, and love that you have poured into me! I would also like to thank my siblings, nieces, and nephews for the love and support that has been shown to me since embarking on this journey. I especially want to personally thank my sister Tanthony and my brother Anthony Jr. for their moral and spiritual support while giving birth to this book.

This project has been a long time coming! A decade ago, I entered graduate school at Michigan State University as a determined teacher-scholar-activist coming to seek justice for the students I mis-educated by way of my own linguistic mis-education. I still remember the very moment that I was inspired to write this book. After listening to me complain in her class about how the literature on Black Language was not reaching classroom teachers in Black school districts like Detroit, Dr. G aka the Jay-Z of Academics (a nickname I gave her when we first met) said, "well, sound like you need to write the book you wanna see in the world!" And here I am, 10 years later, the author of the book that has been missing from the world. I owe much gratitude to you, Dr. G, for your love and commitment to Black people and our Black Language! I thank you for always pouring into me and schooling me and for your continued love and mentorship. This book is for you, G!

Thanks to the students at Leadership Academy for welcoming me into their space and allowing me to learn alongside them. I thank all of the students I have had the pleasure of working with when I taught in Detroit for making my life even more meaningful! This book is for all of y'all!

I am deeply humbled and indebted to the small circle of amazing folk that I kept very close to my writing process: Lamar Johnson, my writing/thinking partner and co-conspirator in this academic game who was always available to read parts of this book no matter the time, day or location. I thank you for the critical feedback and support you provided me throughout this process. I thank you for seeing the vision even when my eyes became too weary to see it for myself. To Carmen Kynard, Eric Pritchard, and David Glisch-Sanchez aka my Takedown Team: Thanks for protecting my writing and my soul throughout this process! The text messages, the memes, the gifs, the laughs, the astrology fights, and the deep conversations about not losing our souls in this academic game did so much good for my heart, my mind, and my spirit. Eric, thank you for the numerous book writing tips you shared and for always inspiring me to write with my ancestors in mind. Carmen, I am eternally grateful for your brilliant, dope, creative, and hilarious feedback! Thanks for inspiring me to make space in this book for that smart mouf lil Black girl from the D that still lives in me. I am forever grateful for Marcelle Haddix, who has been a solid sista and a good friend throughout this process. I thank you for your check-ins, honest feedback, and for always reminding me of the good I bring to this academic space.

I owe many thanks to Valerie Kinloch and Susi Long for seeing the strength in this project and for being patient, protective, and gentle editors. I am grateful to the talented and amazing artist and scholar Grace Player for the paining on the front cover of the book. *Linguistic Justice* would not have been possible without my MA thesis advisor, Doug Baker; my dissertation advisor, David Kirkland, or my dissertation committee members: Denise Troutman and Django Paris. I am grateful for the mentorship I received and the community I developed in Cultivating New Voices Among Scholars of Color (CNV) Fellowship program, the Scholars of Color Transitioning into Academic Research Institutions (STAR) Fellowship program, and the Smitherman-Villanueva Book Retreat. Finally, I am grateful for the brilliant students who read the first draft of *Linguistic Justice* in my spring 2019 Black Language course: Constance Haywood, Chamelia Moore,

Kaelyn Muiru, Floyd Pouncil, Nick Sanders, Daryhl Covington, Dinah George, China Gross, Sheridan Leatherberry, Micah Reed, Erykah Ross, Victor Ruiz-Divas, Frankie Stringer, and Tim Thomas. This is y'all's book too! I also want to offer my warmest thanks to Davena Jackson, Tiffany Whittington, Cyrin Watson, Mimi Hudson, Alice Lee, Elaine Richardson, and Matthew Homrich-Knieling.

1

"BLACK LANGUAGE IS GOOD ON ANY MLK BOULEVARD"

I grew up in the D! My mother tongue, *Black Language*, was the dominant language I came up on. I have always marveled at the way the Black people in my community would *talk that talk*. From *signifying* to *habitual be* to *call and response*, my linguistic community had a way of using language that was powerful, colorful, and unique. My mother still remains my favorite linguistic role model. As a young girl, I would "try-on" my mother's speech styles in conversations with my siblings, friends, or in instances where I needed to protect myself and others. This language, this Black Language, is the language that nurtured and socialized me to understand the world and how to participate in it. Morgan (2015) emphasizes the importance of the mother tongue. She says it is the first language learned as an infant, child, and youth. It is the first source to impart knowledge and insight about language and culture. Growing up, I was fascinated with Black Language and culture. I would often write stories, poems, and cards that were flavored with Black Language. When I was younger, I made my siblings play school, and yes, yours truly was the teacher. My young teachings incorporated writings by Black authors like Maya Angelou, Toni Morrison, Alice Walker, Langston Hughes, and Amiri Baraka. In middle school, I created my own family newsletter that was modeled after JET and Word Up! Magazines. Black Language was never a place of struggle for me. I don't recall any memories of personally being corrected by teachers or my parents telling me to code-switch for opportunity or success, though I would peep my mom and dad "changing their voices" every now and again to sound more white when they were conducting business over the telephone. During my junior year of high school, I remember catching wind of the *Oakland Ebonics Controversy* (Rickford & Rickford, 2000), which created tension within the Black community about the way we talk. I recall overhearing my Black math teacher criticize Black Language by referring to it as poor grammar and ignorant. My parents took a different stance on the issue. They were sick and tired of the relentless shaming of Black people—the way we talk, the way we walk, the way we dress, the way we eat, and the way we live. I was personally unbothered by the debate and the demeaning messages about a language that my lived experiences had already validated. Black Language for me has always reflected Black people's ways of knowing, interpreting, surviving, and being in the world.

Seeing Language in Black and White

Throughout *Linguistic Justice: Black Language, Literacy, Identity, and Pedagogy*, I deliberately use the terms **Black Language** (BL) and **White Mainstream English** (WME) to foreground the relationship between language, race, anti-Black racism, and white linguistic supremacy. It was through my research with Black youth in Detroit that compelled me to begin using terms that more explicitly captured the intersections between language and race. In the study that this book is based on, I did not originally use Black Language or White Mainstream English as language descriptors. Back then, I was still using African American Language in place of Black Language and Dominant American English (DAE) in place of White Mainstream English. The term Dominant American English is another descriptor used in place of standard English or White Mainstream English, and it was coined by Django Paris (2009) to imply power. Even so, when using this term with the Black youth in the study, I found DAE to be a challenging term to use when trying to offer an analysis of linguistic racism. Despite discussions about language and power, it took some of the students a while to understand that DAE was not more important than Black Language. The use of the adjective "dominant" in the descriptor oftentimes reinforced the white linguistic dominance it was intended to deconstruct.

By linking the racial classifications Black and white to language, I am challenging you, the reader, to see how linguistic hierarchies and racial hierarchies are interconnected. That is, people's language experiences are not separate from their racial experiences. Indeed, the way a Black child's language is devalued in school reflects how Black lives are devalued in the world. Similarly, the way a white child's language is privileged and deemed the norm in schools is directly connected to the invisible ways that white culture is deemed normal, neutral, and superior in the world.

Smitherman (2006) describes Black Language as:

> a style of speaking English words with Black Flava—with Africanized semantic, grammatical, pronunciation, and rhetorical patterns. [Black Language] comes out of the experience of U.S. slave descendants. This shared experience has resulted in common language practices in the Black community. The roots of African American speech lie in the counter language, the

resistance discourse, that was created as a communication system unintelligible to speakers of the dominant master class.

(Smitherman, 2006, p. 3)

Labels such as African American Language (AAL), African American English (AAE), Ebonics, African American Vernacular English (AAVE), and many others are used interchangeably with Black Language. I use Black Language intentionally in my scholarship to acknowledge Africologists' theories that maintain that Black speech is the continuation of African in an American context. Africologists argue that Black Language is a language in its own right that includes features of West African Languages, and it is not just a set of deviations from the English Language (Kifano & Smith, 2003). I also use Black Language politically in my scholarship to align with the mission of Black Liberation movements like Black Lives Matter.

> [We are] committed to struggling together and to imagining and creating a world free of anti-Blackness, where every Black person has the social, economic, and political power to thrive. Black Lives Matter began as a call to action in response to state-sanctioned violence and Anti-Black racism. Our intention from the very beginning was to connect Black people from all over the world who have a shared desire for justice to act together in their communities. The impetus for that commitment was, and still is, the rampant and deliberate violence inflicted on us by the state.
>
> *(Black Lives Matter statement)*[1]

No doubt, the *Anti-Black Linguistic Racism* that is used to diminish Black Language and Black students in schools is not separate from the rampant and deliberate anti-Black racism and violence inflicted upon Black people in society. Like the mission of Black Lives Matter, *Linguistic Justice* is a call to action: a call to radically imagine and create a world free of anti-blackness. A call to create an education system where Black students, their language, their literacies, their culture, their creativity, their joy, their imagination, their brilliance, their freedom, their existence, their resistance MATTERS.

Following Alim & Smitherman (2012), I use the term **White Mainstream English** in place of standard English to emphasize how white ways of speaking become the invisible—or better, inaudible—norm. In a conversation with me about how White Mainstream English gets normalized as standard English, raceradical, Black-Feminist-compositionist Carmen Kynard once said:

> WME means something different from standardized English. Many white people think they are speaking standard English when they simply are not; they are just normative so the moniker of standard follows them from the flow of white privilege.

Echoing this school of thought, Smitherman (2006) makes it clear that the only reason White Mainstream English "is the form of English that gets considered 'standard' [is] because it derives from the style of speaking and the language habits of the dominant, race, class, and gender in U.S. society" (p. 6). I discuss White Mainstream English and whiteness more explicitly in chapter 2.

Entering the Language Wars

Despite growing up loving Black Language, I did not develop a full under-standing of language politics until I started teaching English Language Arts (ELA) at a high school on the eastside of Detroit, which is really a damn shame given (1) the legacy of Dr. G aka Geneva Smitherman's pioneering work on Black Language in Detroit and around the world; (2) some of the most influential Black Language research happened in the D (see Wolfram, 1969; also see Smitherman's foreword of this book); and (3) the landmark 1977 Ann Arbor Black English case took place in Ann Arbor, Michigan—only an hour away from where I grew up and taught (see Smitherman, 1981, 2006). There really is not a legit reason why any teacher in the state of Michigan should walk out of a teacher education program unaware and ill-prepared to address Black Language in their classrooms, but here we are! This is why *Linguistic Justice* is personal. I see this book as an opportunity to speak back to my 22-year-old self, a young Black teacher who wanted to enact what bell hooks describes as a revolutionary pedagogy of resis-tance—a way of thinking about pedagogy in relation to the practice of freedom. I would have never imagined that the preparation (or lack thereof) that I received from my teacher education program would contribute to me reproducing the same racial and linguistic inequities I was hoping to dismantle.

To keep it all the way real, I credit my students for my entry into what Dr. G refers to as the "language wars." Just like most Black people who lived in the D, the students I worked with communicated in Black Language as their primary language—it was reflected in their speech and writing. On the one hand, as a speaker of Black Language myself, I recognized that my students were commu-nicating in a language that was valid and necessary at home, in school, and in the hood, but I was receiving pressure from school administrators to get the students to use the "language of school." I personally found this problematic given that the language arts methods that I received from my teacher education program catered to native speakers of White Mainstream English and assumed that every student entering ELA classrooms spoke this way. At that time, I did not have the language to name the white linguistic hegemony that was embedded in our dis-ciplinary discourses, pedagogical practices, and theories of language, nor did I have the tools to engage my students in critical conversations about Anti-Black Linguistic Racism. I can still recall having a conversation with students in one of my ELA classes about code-switching when one of them flat out said, "What I look like using standard English? It don't even sound right." Other students joined in and insinuated that using "standard English" made them feel like they were being forced to "talk white" and many questioned why they had to communicate in a language that was not reflective of their culture or linguistic backgrounds. My own cultural competence as a Black Language-speaker knew my students were speaking nothing but the TRUTH, but as a classroom teacher, I was ill-equipped to address the critical linguistic issues that they were raising. What I learned early on in my teaching career was that many of my Black students resisted the standard language ideology because they felt it reflected white linguistic and cultural norms, and some of them were not interested in imitating a culture they did not consider themselves to be a part of.

As I continued my teaching journey, I became interested in understanding the language wars outside the contexts of my own experiences. I visited other schools and classrooms in Detroit and its surrounding areas to inquire about how other teachers were responding pedagogically to their Black students' language practices. I learned that some classrooms operated as cultural and linguistic battlegrounds instead of havens where students' language practices were affirmed, valued, and sustained. I listened to stories from teachers who faulted, punished, and belittled their students for showing up to school with a language that was deemed incompatible with the literacy conventions expected in the academic setting. As I compared these practices to the counterstories I was hearing from Black students about the deficit and culturally irrelevant language education they were receiving in schools, I found it important to speak back to these injustices by working at the intersections of theory and praxis.

"You On The Wrong Side of History, Bro." *Linguistic Justice* Is For Teachers Like You!

> In order to dismantle white supremacy, we have to teach students to code-switch!—Teacher
>
> If y'all actually believe that using "standard English" will dismantle white supremacy, then you not paying attention! If we, as teachers, truly believe that code-switching will dismantle white supremacy, we have a problem. If we honestly believe that code-switching will save Black people's lives, then we really ain't paying attention to what's happening in the world. Eric Garner was choked to death by a police officer while saying "I cannot breathe." Wouldn't you consider "I cannot breathe" "standard English" syntax? —Baker-Bell

This heated exchange occurred during a presentation that I co-facilitated with four of my former students (now classroom teachers) at the 2017 National Council of Teachers of English (NCTE) annual convention. For those of y'all who don't know, NCTE is one of the most celebrated, long-standing professional organizations for English teachers, and it prides itself and its members on using the power of language and literacy to actively pursue justice and equity for all students. Yet, there I was in a session where some of the organization's members were representing and advocating for a racist, punitive, anti-Black youth kind of linguistic politics. Let me paint a bigger picture of the problem: NCTE and its constituent, Conference on College Composition and Communication (CCCC), has been "a forum for linguistic debates and language issues of various kinds" since the early 1950s (Smitherman, 2003). In 1974, NCTE/CCCC adopted the Students' Right to Their Own Language (SRTOL) resolution, which states:

> We affirm the students' right to their own patterns and varieties of language—the dialects of their nurture or whatever dialects in which they find their own identity and style. Language scholars long ago denied that the myth of a standard American dialect has any validity. The claim that any one dialect is unacceptable amounts to an attempt of one social group to exert its dominance over another. Such a claim leads to false advice for speakers and writers, and immoral advice for humans. A nation proud of its diverse heritage and its cultural and racial variety will preserve its heritage of dialects. We affirm strongly that teachers must have the experiences and training that will enable them to respect diversity and uphold the right of students to their own language.
>
> *(Students' Right, 1974)*

Yet, nearly seven decades later, we still have English teachers out here perpetuating and advocating for Anti-Black Linguistic Racism. Now let's circle back to what happened during the presentation. The presentation was supposed to illuminate how teachers can work against racial and linguistic inequities in their classrooms. The exchange happened after one of my former students provided attendees with the sociolinguistic receipts that showed the validity of Black Language, and she illustrated how so-called "standard English" is a hypothetical construct. During the activity that followed, a young Black teacher stated that while he agrees that teachers should do more to value Black Language in the classroom, in order to dismantle white supremacy, we have to teach students to code-switch. I was not surprised by what the young man said because many teachers do not realize that standard English is a byproduct of white supremacy. It also did not surprise me that this sentiment was coming out of the mouth of a Black teacher. Internalized anti-Blackness is REAL, and it will have you on the frontlines reinforcing a system of white supremacy and upholding racist policies and practices that legitimize your own suffering and demise. Elaine Richardson aka Docta E said it best in a Facebook post, "white supremacy lives in all of us, but we all ought to be tryna unlearn white supremacy." What was troublesome to me, especially given the current racial and social climate in the U.S., was that he is probably telling his Black students that "standard English" could dismantle white supremacy or save Black people's lives. I'm not sure if I was more upset because the young teacher who said this was Black and miseducated or if it was because he said this in a room full of white teachers who seemed to have felt a sense of relief by his comment. My point here is that the white teachers in the room could use this Black teacher's anti-Black sentiments as justification for racist language policies, practices, pedagogies, and classrooms. This is one of many examples that underscores the need for *Black Linguistic Consciousness*, and it is the impetus for this book.

"We Want to Be Linguistically Free Too": What Do I Mean by Linguistic Justice?

In her book, *Cultivating Racial and Linguistic Diversity in Literacy Teacher Education: Teachers Like Me*, Marcelle Haddix (2015) argues that the notion of social justice has become a co-opted term—a buzz word—among teacher education researchers. No doubt! I think this is an important critique, and as a teacher-scholar-activist, it is essential that I discuss what I mean by Linguistic Justice. *Linguistic Justice,* the book and the framework, is about Black Language and Black Liberation. It is an antiracist approach to language and literacy education. It is about dismantling Anti-Black Linguistic Racism and white linguistic hegemony and supremacy in classrooms and in the world. As a pedagogy, Linguistic Justice places Black Language at the center of Black students' language education and experiences. Linguistic Justice does not see White Mainstream English as the be-all and end-all for Black speakers. Linguistic Justice does not side-step fairness and freedom. Instead, it affords Black students the same kinds of linguistic liberties that are afforded to white students. Within a Linguistic Justice framework, excuses such as "that's just the way it is" cannot be used as justification for Anti-Black Linguistic Racism, white linguistic supremacy, and linguistic injustice. Telling children that White Mainstream English is needed for survival can no longer be the answer, especially as we are witnessing Black people being mishandled, discriminated against, and murdered while using White Mainstream English, and in some cases, before they even open their mouths.

"Stylin' and Profilin'": A Black Language Theoreticum

The style and organization of *Linguistic Justice* is just as important as its contents, and it reflects how Black Language lives in my life. I assembled the book using a collection of images, dialogues, charts, graphs, instructional maps, images, artwork, stories, and weblinks to capture the multifaceted ways that I see, understand, and interact with Black Language on a daily basis. Indeed, engaging in multimodal practices provided me with space to fully capture the richness, complexity, and dynamism of Black Language. *Linguistic Justice* also pushes the boundaries of many academic book genres by remixing multiple modes and styles of writing. While reading, the book might feel like a manifesto, a theory reader, and a collection of critical praxis—all within one book. As a result, I present *Linguistic Justice* as a Black Language Theoreticum, a theory meets practicum book. This book also pushes beyond the limitations of what teachers have traditionally called lesson plans. Referring to the learning experiences that I curated for the students as lesson plans will have teachers reducing the *Antiracist Black Language Pedagogy* to a step-by-step guide to language instruction versus a commitment to eradicating Anti-Black Linguistic Racism. As such, I share the learning experiences that I curated as Black Language Artifacts of my Antiracist Black Language Pedagogy.

Linguistic Justice is a teacher-scholar-activist project I did with young people in Detroit that explored their experiences navigating and negotiating their linguistic and racial identities across multiple contexts. In particular, the book reveals how traditional approaches to language education do not account for the emotional harm or consequences these approaches have on Black students' sense of self and identity. In the book, I offer Anti-Black Linguistic Racism as a framework that explicitly names and richly captures the type of linguistic oppression that is uniquely experienced and endured by Black Language-speakers. In response to this, I introduce Antiracist Black Language Pedagogy, a pedagogy that comprises of seven critical inquiry-based learning experiences that provided Black students with an opportunity to learn Black Language, learn through Black Language, and learn about Black Language (Halliday, 1993) while simultaneously working toward dismantling Anti-Black Linguistic Racism.

In chapter 2, I offer Anti-Black Linguistic Racism as a framework that helps explain precisely how Anti-Black Linguistic Racism gets normalized in and through our research, disciplinary discourses, curricular choices, pedagogical practices. This chapter also shows how damaging these decisions are on Black students' language education and their racial and linguistic identities. I then theorize and offer some framing ideas for what I am terming Antiracist Black Language Pedagogy as an approach that confronts Anti-Black Linguistic Racism in teacher attitudes, curriculum and instruction, pedagogical approaches, disciplinary discourse, and research.

Chapter 3 centers the voices and counterstories of the Black students I worked with. I illustrate how listening to their stories and linguistic experiences counter the dominant narrative about what Black students need in a language education. Their counterstories affirm that eradicationist and respectability approaches to Black Language education do not account for the emotional harm, internalized Anti-Black Linguistic Racism, or consequences these approaches have on Black students' sense of self and identity. I argue in this chapter that Black Language-speakers' voices and stories matter! And as educators and researchers, we must listen and engage their perspectives in our research, theories of language learning, and in our pedagogical practices.

In chapter 4, I show the praxis of the Antiracist Black Language Pedagogy, specifically illustrating how I used Black Linguistic Consciousness-raising to help the students challenge, interrogate, unlearn, and work toward dismantling Anti-

Black Linguistic Racism. This chapter has two major functions: (1) it demonstrates what an Antiracist Black Language Pedagogy looks like on the ground (aka in the classroom); and (2) it illustrates how theory, research, and practice can operate in tandem in pursuit of linguistic and racial justice.

Chapter 5 presents composite character counterstories that reflect how the students were beginning to develop a Black Linguistic Consciousness following the Antiracist Black Language Pedagogy. This chapter also offers implications that highlight the necessity of an Antiracist Black Language Pedagogy in our current historical, political, and racial climate.

Finally, chapter 6 functions like a bonus chapter. It was not part of the study that I describe in chapters 2–5, but it illustrates how I use Angie Thomas' book *The Hate U Give* to approach Antiracist Black Language Pedagogy in my English education courses for preservice teachers. Through several Black Language Artifacts, I show how African American literature can provide a rich foundation for students to explore how identity is conceived through language expression and how African American literature is an important vehicle to work toward dismantling Anti-Black Linguistic Racism.

Note

1 Black Lives Matter website, https://blacklivesmatter.com/

References

Alim, H. S., & Smitherman, G. (2012). *Articulate While Black: Barack Obama, Language, and Race in the U.S.* Oxford, NY: Oxford University Press.

Haddix, M. (2015). *Cultivating Racial and Linguistic Diversity in Literacy Teacher Education: Teachers Like Me*. New York, NY, & Urbana, IL: Routledge & National Council of Teachers of English.

Halliday, M. A. K. (1993). Towards a language-based theory of learning. *Linguistics and Education*, 5(2), 93–116.

Kifano, S., & Smith, E. (2003). Ebonics and education in the context of culture: Meeting the language and cultural needs of LEP African American students. In J. Ramirez, T. Wiley, G. de Klerk, E. Lee, & W. Wright, (Eds), *Ebonics: The Urban Education Debate*. England: Multilingual Matters LTD.

Morgan, M. (2015). African American women's language: Mother tongues untied. In S. Lanehart, *The Oxford Handbook of African American Language* (pp. 817–833). New York, NY: Oxford University Press.

Paris, D. (2009). They're in my culture, they speak the same way: African American language in multiethnic high schools. *Harvard Educational Review*, 79(3), 428–448.

Rickford, J. R., & Rickford, R. J. (2000). *Spoken Soul: The Story of Black English*. New York, NY: Wiley.

Smitherman, G. (1981). "What go round come round": King in perspective. In *Talkin That Talk: African American Language and Culture* (pp. 133–149). New York, NY: Routledge.

Smitherman, G. (2006). *Word From the Mother: Language and African Americans.* New York, NY: Routledge.

Smitherman, G., & Villanueva, V. (2003). *Language Diversity in the Classroom: From Intention to Practice.* Carbondale, IL: Southern Illinois University Press.

Students' Right to Their Own Language (1974). *College, Composition and Communication.* 25(3), 1–32.

Wolfram, W. (1969). *A Sociolinguistic Description of Detroit Negro Speech.* Washington, DC: Center for Applied Linguistics.

2

"WHAT'S ANTI-BLACKNESS GOT TO DO WIT IT?"

It's not just about language or the way you talk.

—*Janel, Leadership Academy*

Many of the youth I worked with at Leadership Academy, like Janel, depicted their experiences navigating and negotiating their racial and linguistic identities across multiple contexts in deeply complex and nuanced ways. On the one hand, as illustrated in chapter 3, many of the youth viewed Black Language as a vital linguistic resource in their communities and classrooms. Yet, many of the same youth shared stories of their experiences with what I am referring to as ***Anti-Black Linguistic Racism*** in these very same contexts. The youths' experiences with Anti-Black Linguistic Racism elucidate Michael Eric Dyson's (2009) sentiments about the relationship between Black Language and Black humanity: "Every conversation about Black speech is a conversation about Black intelligence and ultimately Black humanity" (p. 1). The question that I want you to keep in mind as you read this chapter is: What is the relationship between anti-Black racism and Black Language?

Anti-Black Linguistic Racism describes the linguistic violence, persecution, dehumanization, and marginalization that Black Language-speakers experience in schools and in everyday life. The Anti-Black Linguistic Racism that the youth at Leadership Academy, as well as countless other Black people, experience and endure in communities and classrooms is not separate from the contemporary forms of anti-Black racism and oppression they encounter as they navigate the world living within their Black bodies. Indeed, the marginalization, colonization, exploitation, policing, and stereotypes associated with Black Language is linked to a system of white supremacy that continues to support and maintain "the oppression, exploitation, and overall domination of all Black people" (hooks,

1992, p. 2) and other people of color. Thus, the policing of Black Language and literacies in schools is not separate from the ways in which Black bodies have historically been policed and surveilled in U.S. society, and the ubiquitous assault and murder of Black bodies is not independent of the symbolic linguistic violence and spirit-murder that Black students experience daily in classrooms (Bryan, 2020; Johnson et al., 2017; Johnson, 2018; Love, 2019). This is important to note since linguistic racism and oppression, especially as experienced by Black people, tend to get overlooked or are undertheorized in broader critical race scholarship and pedagogies. Indeed, folks will argue until they are blue in the face about anti-Black racism, but once language is brought into the equation, those same people will say "you have to use the master's tool (or language) to dismantle the master's house." In the words of Audre Lorde (1984), "the master's tools will never dismantle the master's house" (p. 1).

In this chapter, I offer Anti-Black Linguistic Racism as a framework that explicitly names and richly captures the type of linguistic oppression that is uniquely experienced and endured by Black Language-speakers. This framework also helps explain precisely how Anti-Black Linguistic Racism gets normalized in and through our research, disciplinary discourses, curricular choices, pedagogical practices, and teacher attitudes, and it shows how damaging these decisions are on Black students' language education and racial and linguistic identities. I then theorize and offer some framing ideas for what I am terming *Antiracist Black Language Pedagogy* as an approach that confronts Anti-Black Linguistic Racism in teacher attitudes, curriculum and instruction, pedagogical approaches, disciplinary discourse, and research.

"If You Don't Know Now Ya Know": A Brief Breakdown of Black Language

Despite decades of research on Black Language, its survival since enslavement, and its linguistic imprint on the nation and globe (Smitherman, 2006), Black people and Black Language scholars keep having to remind y'all that it is a legit language. James Baldwin (1979) said it best in the *New York Times*, "If Black English isn't a language, then tell me, what is?" From a purely linguistic standpoint, like "every naturally used language, [Black Language] is systematic with regular rules at the lexical, phonological, and grammatical level" (Stanford University, 2002, p. 1). I take a close look at the history of Black Language and its features in chapters 4 and 5, but I offer an abbreviated breakdown here in order to contextualize Anti-Black Linguistic Racism. As stated in chapter 1, Smitherman (2006) describes Black Language as:

> a style of speaking English words with Black Flava—with Africanized semantic, grammatical, pronunciation, and rhetorical patterns. [Black Language] comes out of the experience of U.S. slave descendants. This shared

experience has resulted in common language practices in the Black community. The roots of African American speech lie in the counter language, the resistance discourse, that was created as a communication system unintelligible to speakers of the dominant master class.

(Smitherman, 2006, p. 3)

Black Language is the rhetoric of resistance embedded in the hashtag #BlackLivesMatter, which led to the birth of what some call the 21st century civil rights movement. It is the phonology and grammatical structure former president Barack Obama used when declining to accept change from a Black cashier by saying, "*Nah, we straight.*" Black Language is the controversial words of wisdom that Michelle Obama shared at the 2016 Democratic National Convention, "*When they go low, we go high.*" It is the blackness reflected in the style of speech that "woke" CNN political commentator and NPR political analyst Angela Rye unabashedly and unapologetically uses on national news to clap back and break down racial oppression *for the people in the back*. Black Language is the linguistic inventiveness and signification in the infamous three-word response "*Reclaiming My Time*" that Congresswoman Maxine Waters used to drag U.S. Treasury Secretary Steve Mnuchin, after he dodged her questions and spoke over her during a committee hearing in 2017. It is the rhetorical strategies that Tiana Smalls, a Black woman, used to prevent Border Patrol officers from illegally searching a greyhound bus and demanding that passengers show their documentation. Black Language is also the native language and rich linguistic resources that so many Black children bring into classrooms every day.

But let us not forget—Black Language is also the language that continuously gets appropriated, exploited, and colonized. Since I began my research on Black Language in 2008, I have collected numerous examples of **Black linguistic appropriation** and the ways Black Language and literacies have been capitalized on. Some of the recent examples include the 2017 Mountain Dew commercial that used rappers Fat Joe, Remy Ma, and French Montana's song *I'm All the Way Up* [1] to promote their product and Party City's 2018 commercial using rapper DMX's song *Party Up (Up In Here)* [2] to promote their unicorn party theme. MARS Incorporated also used the Black lexical slang item "cray cray" to personalize their snicker wrappers in 2015, and MTV culturally appropriated Black Language in an article written in 2016 by encouraging its mostly white viewers to stop using Black slang words that were popular in 2015 and start using new Black slang words in 2016.[3] Trader Joe's capitalized on Black Language when the neighborhood grocer used "Oh, Snap" to advertise their asparagus. Many fashion designers have also capitalized on Black Language to create market messages to invite consumers to buy their products. I cannot tell you how many times I have walked into retail stores that sold tee shirts, mugs, hats, and pillows that have capitalized on and appropriated Black Language (see Figure 2.1). Jay Z said it best: "the mainstream done crossed over to us" (Alim & Smitherman, 2012,

FIGURE 2.1 Examples of Black Linguistic Appropriation

p. 361). Yet, as shown in chapter 3, in classrooms, Black Language is devalued and viewed as a symbol of linguistic and intellectual inferiority. So essentially what this says is: It is acceptable for Black Language to be used and capitalized on by non-native Black Language-speakers for marketing and for play, but it is unacceptable for Black kids to use it as a linguistic resource in school. This is unfortunate but unsurprising because Black Language is one of those features of Black culture that white America loves to hate, yet loves to take.[4] This is why we need to be talkin' about Anti-Black Linguistic Racism.

On Linguistic Racism

Several sociolinguists and language scholars have discussed, theorized, and analyzed how linguistic discrimination gets supported and maintained through institutional practices. For instance, Lippi-Green (2012) very pointedly illustrates how the process of language subordination is achieved through what she refers to as the *standard language ideology*:

> The standard language ideology (SLI) is a bias toward an abstracted, idealized, homogenous spoken language which is imposed and maintained by dominant bloc institutions and which names as its model the written language, but which is drawn primarily from the spoken language of the upper middle class.
>
> *(Lippi-Green, 2012, p. 67)*

The standard language ideology goes unquestioned in our institutions, particularly in schools, as a result of the disinformation and misrepresentation that get distributed about dominant languages and marginalized languages and dialects. Wiley's (2000) definition of linguistic hegemony is useful in showing how institutions are successful in convincing linguistically marginalized communities to buy into the supremacy of a language that is not their own:

> Linguistic hegemony is achieved when dominant groups create a consensus by convincing others to accept their language norms and usage as standard or paradigmatic. Hegemony is ensured when they can convince those who fail to meet those standards to view their failure as being the result of the inadequacy of their own language.
>
> *(Wiley, 2000, p. 11)*

Despite the persistence of linguistic hegemony, "linguistic science does not recognize any language or dialect as inherently superior or inferior to any other" (Lippi-Green, 2012 p. 33).

Linguistic hegemony and the standard language ideology are useful frameworks in making sense of how language subordination works between dominant and marginalized groups; however, neither framework offers an explicit analysis of linguistic racism or the role that race plays in language subordination. Now make no mistake—I ain't saying that these linguists have not discussed these frameworks in relation to linguistically marginalized communities of color. For instance, Lippi-Green (2012) keeps it real about the relationship between language and race when she states, "a standard language ideology ... attempts to justify rejection of the other because of race, ethnicity or other facets of identity that would otherwise be called racism" (p. 74), and Alim, Rickford, and Ball (2016) acknowledge that "the relationship between language, race, and culture has long been a topic of interest in linguistic anthropology" (p. 3). However, these affirmations are not explicit in many of our guiding frameworks, which could contribute to language scholars and literacy educators ignoring the relationship between language and race. Though this book centers Black Language, it is important to note that Anti-Black Linguistic Racism is part of a larger system of white linguistic and cultural hegemony that advances the needs, self-interests, and racial privileges of whites at the expense of linguistically marginalized communities of color. No doubt, so-called "standard" English is "the language of conquest and domination; in the United States, it is the mask which hides the loss of so many tongues, all those sounds of diverse, native communities we will never hear" (hooks, 1994, p. 168). Building on Delgado and Stefancic's (2017) definition of racism, I understand linguistic racism as any system or practice of discrimination, segregation, persecution, or mistreatment of language based on membership in a race or ethnic group. From a Critical Race Theory perspective, linguistic racism is normal and an everyday experience for most linguistically marginalized people of color living in the U.S. In fact, it is so normal that it is difficult to address because it is not acknowledged as a form of racism. And although linguistic racism is socially constructed, like racism, it is permanent and ubiquitous in U.S. society. That is, as long as racism is an issue, we'll always have linguistic racism, despite pedagogies that promise speaking White Mainstream English will save linguistically marginalized people of color.

Scholars in the emerging field of raciolinguistics (Alim, Rickford, & Ball, 2016; Flores & Rosa, 2015; Alim & Smitherman, 2012) argue that we need more explicit critical analytical tools that examine what it means to speak as a racialized subject, especially in hyperracial times. This is a salient point because without analyzing language through the lens of race and racism, we ignore how linguistic violence and racial violence go hand in hand. Furthermore, ignoring the relationship between language and race contributes to us missing the mark as far as examining language-focused discrimination from an intersectional standpoint, which offers insight into how communities of color experience linguistic discrimination differently than white linguistically marginalized communities. For example, an indigenous child who communicates in an indigenous language, a Black child who communicates in Black Language, a Latinx child who communicates in Spanglish, and an Asian American child who communicates in Asian American English, will experience linguistic discrimination differently from a white child who communicates in Appalachian English. This is because children of color's experiences navigating and negotiating language will be impacted by the interlocking systems and structures of linguicism, racism, and classism, which are interrelated and continuously shaping one another. Failing to theorize about language through the lens of race also contributes to us missing opportunities to critique, expand, and improve our theories of language and language pedagogies, which oftentimes perpetuate linguistic racism and uphold white linguistic supremacy.

Theorizing language through the lens of race provides insightful historical and political analyses of how linguistic racism has been institutionalized. For instance, despite anti-discrimination laws that were passed and intended to make it no longer permissible to outright use race to legally discriminate in employment, housing, education, courts, and in everyday life (though it still goes down), new tactics have been crafted in support of racial exclusion and discrimination. Instead of explicitly using the color of someone's skin, for example, more subtle approaches to racism, such as language-focused racism, have been used to exclude and discriminate against linguistically and racially diverse groups. Lippi-Green (2012) posits:

> We do not, cannot under our laws ask a person to change the color of their skin, her religion, her gender, her sexual identity, but we regularly demand of people that they suppress or deny the most effective way they have of situating themselves socially in the world.
>
> *(Lippi-Green, 2012, p. 66)*

Indeed, there are no explicit laws in the U.S. that make it illegal to use one's language as justification for discrimination and exclusion, and therefore, "language and accent have become an acceptable excuse to publicly turn away, to refuse to recognize the other or acknowledge their rights" (Lippi-Green, 2012, p. 67). For example, Black Language "has become an even more important vehicle in the denial of access to resources to Blacks, particularly in housing" (Alim & Smitherman, 2012, p. 54). And although there is no official language in the U.S., there is a long and well-documented history of institutionalized linguistic racism via English-Only policies that have marginalized and disenfranchised Spanish-speaking populations (Anzaldua, 1987; Lippi-Green, 2012). Following the 2016 election of Donald Trump, there has been an increase in linguistic racism toward Spanish-speaking populations. During his campaign, Trump was noted as saying "This is a country where we speak English, not Spanish." In May 2018, Aaron Schlossberg, a Manhattan attorney, was videoed insulting staff at a New York deli and threatening to call Immigration and Customs Enforcement (ICE) because the workers were speaking in Spanish, not English. These contemporary forms of linguistic racism further reveal why it is important "to ask and answer critical questions about the relations between language, race, and power" (Alim, Rickford, & Ball, 2016, p. 3).

Although raciolinguistics and other frameworks that theorize language and race are critical and necessary for a general analysis of linguistic racism, we also need frameworks that offer explicit "more detailed, nuanced, historicized, and embodied theorizations [of each linguistically marginalized communities of color racial and linguistic] conditions under specific formations of racial oppression" (Dumas & ross, 2016, p. 417). Pertaining to Black Language-speakers, Baugh (2000) argues that "substantial linguistic evidence indicates that slave descendants of African origin should not be equated with US immigrants" (p. 37). Building on this point, he also states:

> When compared to the linguistic circumstances of United States immigrants who hailed from Italy, Germany, France, Poland, Sweden, Russia, Japan, China, Korea, Mexico, Brazil, and countless other countries, slaves never had

the luxury of being able to speak to others using their native language once they were brought to America—again, against their free will. Secondly, but crucially from a linguistic point of view, it was illegal to teach slaves to read and write. Thus, in addition to the linguistic isolation that resulted from being captured in Africa and prevention from interacting with others who shared a common African language, once sold in America slaves were intentionally denied access to literacy by law. Traditional immigrants had the advantage—and it is a clear advantage—to speak their native language with others who also immigrated from their heritage country. The vast majority of immigrants who chose to come to the United States were allowed to attend school, where they were introduced to academic varieties of English.

(Baugh, 2015, p. 293)

So not only were enslaved Africans racially segregated, they were linguistically segregated too. Essentially, Baugh is arguing that Black Language is the linguistic consequence of slavery from which linguistic racism toward Black people was born. This historical linguistic record of Black Language illustrates how a general theory of linguistic racism is inadequate in its ability to fully interrogate anti-blackness in and through language. Thus, we need frameworks that interrogate and examine the specific linguistic oppressions experienced by linguistically marginalized communities of color and account for the critical distinctions between their linguistic histories, heritages, experiences, circumstances, and relationships to white supremacy. My hope with Anti-Black Linguistic Racism is that it will move us beyond general theories of linguistic racism and offer a Black theorization of linguistic racism that is necessary to examine how Black people, specifically Black students, experience linguistic oppression in an anti-Black, white supremacist education system and society.

"It's Not Just About Language Or The Way You Talk": Why We Need a Theory of Language That Centers Anti-Blackness

I opened this chapter with a message from Janel, one of the Black girls I worked with at Leadership Academy. During an interview about her experiences speaking Black Language, Janel explained, "it's not just about language or the way you talk." What I learned from working with Janel and many of the Black students I have come to know through my teaching and research was that many of the encounters they had when using Black Language reflected anti-blackness; however, they did not have the precise language to name what they were experiencing, and for a long time, neither did I. While many of the students suspected that their language was oftentimes disregarded due them being Black, they had a difficult time trying to explain and make sense of how one could experience racism through their language. Their confusion about the relationship between language and race points to the necessity of an Antiracist Black Language

Pedagogy that provides students with space to examine how language, race, white supremacy, and anti-blackness intersect and how they can work against Anti-Black Linguistic Racism. I will return to my framework of Antiracist Black Language Pedagogy later in this chapter, but before doing so, I want to discuss how BlackCrit informs my understanding of Anti-Black Linguistic Racism and why this framework is needed to inform our theories of language.

In the field of education, Dumas and ross (2016) developed BlackCrit, a theorization of Black critical theory, as a framework that helps us more precisely examine how Black children are marginalized, disdained, and disregarded in schools and educational spaces. In particular, the authors maintain that:

> BlackCrit in education promises to help us more incisively analyze how social and education policy are informed by antiblackness, and serve as forms of anti-Black violence, and following from this, how these policies facilitate and legitimize Black suffering in the everyday life of schools.
>
> *(Dumas & ross, 2016, p. 419)*

Like other racialized crits (TribalCrit, LatCrit, and AsianCrit), BlackCrit proliferated in response to Ladson-Billing's and Tate's (1995) explication of Critical Race Theory (CRT) in education. As a general theory of racism, CRT functions as an important tool that helps analyze race and racism and critique white supremacy, but it does not precisely name or adequately address the racial oppressions of specific racialized groups (Dumas & ross, 2016). Though CRT is often perceived as a Black critical theory and an analytical tool that is applicable and limited to Black people, Dumas and ross (2016) explains that "it is not a theorization of blackness or even the Black condition; it is a theory of race, or more precisely, racism" (p. 416). Hence, BlackCrit is necessary to confront:

> the specificity of anti-Blackness, as a social construction, as an embodied lived experience of social suffering and resistance, and perhaps most importantly, as an antagonism, in which the Black is despised thing-in-itself in opposition to all that is pure, humane, and white.
>
> *(Dumas & ross, 2016, pp. 416–417)*

In relation to Black Language, BlackCrit helps to show how the linguistic violence, persecution, dehumanization, and marginalization that Black Language-speakers experience in schools and in everyday life are informed by anti-Blackness.

In their theorization of BlackCrit, Dumas and ross note that addressing anti-blackness is different than addressing racism and white supremacy. I want to underscore this point, specifically as it pertains to language education. Much of the language education that students receive in their K-12 and postsecondary education is based on white supremacist values. That is, White Mainstream English (white linguistic and cultural values) is used as the gold standard in which all students are expected to meet. The concept of *Whiteness* is important in understanding the silent and invisible ways in which White Mainstream English serves as the unstated norm in our classrooms (Pimentel, 2011). Alim and Smitherman (2012) break this down in the passage below:

> Whites can exercise power through overt (obvious) and covert (hidden) racist practices. The fact that it is the language and communicative norms of those in power, in any society, that tend to be labeled as "standard", "official", "normal", "appropriate", "respectful", and so on, often goes unrecognized, particularly by the members of the dominating group. In our case, White Mainstream English and White ways of speaking become the invisible—or better, inaudible—norms of what educators and uncritical scholars like to call academic English, the language of school, the language of power, or communicating in academic settings.
>
> *(Alim & Smitherman, 2012, p. 171)*

Elsewhere (Baker-Bell, 2017) I've written about how the ubiquity of whiteness in schools erroneously positions White Mainstream English-speaking students as academically prepared to achieve because their cultural ways of being, their language, their literacies, their histories, their values, and their knowledges are privileged in classrooms. From this assumption, linguistically marginalized students of color are falsely positioned as linguistically inadequate because their language practices do not reflect White Mainstream English.

Certainly, a critique of white supremacy and linguistic racism within language education is important and timely in order to illustrate how our education system privileges and caters to whites at the expense of people of color; however, this critique alone does not fully explain how our language education contributes to "the debasement of black humanity, utter indifference to black suffering, and the denial of Black people's right to exist" (Jeffries as cited in Baker-Bell, Jones Stanbrough, & Everett, 2017). What I am referring to as Anti-Black Linguistic Racism is more than an examination of white linguistic hegemony and how it informs Black students' language education. As Jeffries (2014) explains, "the 'anti' in 'anti-Blackness' is the denial of Black people's right to life" (p. 1). With this in mind, Anti-Black Linguistic Racism more accurately captures the dehumanization that Black Language-speakers endure when using their language across multiple contexts, including classrooms, and it details the ways that anti-Blackness in language education positions Black Language-speaking students as linguistically, intellectually, and morally inferior (Alim & Smitherman, 2012).

Examples of Anti-Black Linguistic Racism includes, but is not limited to, teachers rejecting and not preserving the rich linguistic resources that Black students bring with them to classrooms. It is when Black witnesses, like Rachel Jeantel, have their testimonies disregarded or viewed as insufficient in the criminal justice system due to their use of Black Language (Baugh & King, 2016). It consists of teachers entering classrooms with little to no knowledge about the linguistic and cultural practices their Black students bring with them into classrooms. It includes teachers silencing, correcting, and policing students when they communicate in Black Language. Anti-Black Linguistic Racism is denying Black students the right to use their native language as a linguistic resource in their language and literacy learning. It is insisting that Black students code-switch to avoid discrimination, which essentially penalizes Black students for the existence of Anti-Black Linguistic Racism. It involves teachers believing that there is something inherently wrong with Black Language, and therefore, it must be eradicated. It is requiring Black students to reject their language and culture to acquire White Mainstream English. It is research about Black Language that is disembodied from Black students' lived experiences and how they navigate the world in their Black bodies. As I will illustrate in chapter 3, Anti-Black Linguistic Racism names the dehumanization Black students at Leadership Academy experienced when using Black Language in school. In Table 2.1, I highlight other examples of Anti-Black Linguistic Racism and how it gets normalized in and through teacher attitudes, our curriculum and instruction, our pedagogical approaches to language, and through our research and disciplinary discourses.

The Impact of Anti-Black Linguistic Racism on Black Students

It goes without saying that Anti-Black Linguistic Racism is dangerous and harmful to Black students and their language education, but the harm goes beyond education. Richardson (2004) argues that when "Black students [are] taught to hate Black speech, [it] indirectly [teaches] them to hate themselves" (p. 161). This is the dehumanization that *Linguistic Justice* is concerned with and the problem that Anti-Black Linguistic Racism helps to name in an effort to show how Black children are marginalized, disdained, and disregarded in schools and educational spaces in and through their language. While my research at Leadership Academy taught me that Black students find creative ways to resist anti-blackness and Anti-Black Linguistic Racism, it also revealed how the students internalized anti-Black messages about their language and the consequences this had on their sense of self and identity. An anti-Black Language education not only contributes to Black students despising their mother tongue, but it also causes them to see themselves through a white gaze—"a way of looking and seeing the world that negates [their] value" (hooks, 1992, p. 3). Charity Hudley and Mallison (2014) contend that "speakers who face microaggressions, prejudice, and discrimination also react with internalization, a process whereby members of a stigmatized group accept negative messages about their self-worth" (p. 65).

I write more about this in chapter 3, but I want to briefly highlight the ways this internalization of white supremacist values and anti-blackness was evident in the first activity I had the students at Leadership Academy complete. I asked them to read samples of Black Language and White Mainstream English and draw images of who

TABLE 2.1 How Anti-Black Linguistic Racism is Perpetuated in Education

Teacher Attitudes	<ul><li>Assumptions that Black students are linguistically, morally, and intellectually inferior because they communicate in Black Language.</li><li>Belief that there is something inherently wrong with Black Language and its speakers.</li><li>Belief that Black students' language practices reflect incompetence and a lack of intelligence.</li><li>Belief that Black students must eradicate Black Language to succeed in school and life.</li></ul>Examples of teacher attitudes about Black Language which reflects Anti-Black Linguistic Racism:<ul><li>*"Although he speaks in a non-eloquent way, he is really smart."*— teacher from previous study</li><li>*"My assumption about people who speak this way [Black Language] is that they are from a lower-class and are uneducated"*—from a teacher at a Black Language workshop</li><li>*"I cringe when I hear my students speak like that! It brings out the grammar nazi that lives in me."*—a teacher from a Black Language workshop</li></ul>
Curriculum/Instruction	<ul><li>Black Language is not acknowledged in the curriculum or in the study of language as a valid, rule-based linguistic system.</li><li>Black students are not formally taught the rules of their own language in schools.</li><li>Black Language is ignored or taught uncritically when engaging Black Literature (*Tears of a Tiger, The Hate U Give, Their Eyes Were Watching GOD*, etc.) or literary texts that encompass Black Language-speaking characters (*To Kill a Mockingbird*).</li></ul>Examples of teachers describing their instruction of Black Language which reflects Anti-Black Linguistic Racism:<ul><li>*"One of the goals this year was to get kids to stop sayin … he was, she was"* —teacher from Alim & Smitherman (2012) study (p. 172)</li><li>*"More than a few of my students would turn [in] papers with AAL [African American Language]littered throughout. I would constantly correct their grammar while talking in class [and] make them read aloud so they could get used to hearing the correct ways to speak and write. I think it gave them a reference. It also got me to stop embarrassing people in front of the class."*—teacher from a previous study</li><li>*"I get that people from different cultures and backgrounds communicate differently with each other, but I also understand that my students will enter a land where they will be judged based on their language. Whether this is fair or not, as their teacher, isn't it my job to prepare my Black students to communicate in 'standard English' so that they don't get discriminated against?"*—teacher from a previous study</li></ul>

(Continued)

TABLE 2.1 (*Cont.*)

	• *"I would correct the students and try to get them to speak the 'right way'; can the child know when to speak correctly and be able to show that with academic writing"—preservice teacher from previous study*
	• *"I would probably tell them to try and focus on talking more appropriately; use school language to talk in class and save the slang for lunch and outside of school; I would correct if they wrote like this and try to help them talk properly"—preservice teacher from previous study*
Pedagogy	• **Code-Switching Approach**: a color-evasiveness approach that teaches students to use language to fit the time, place, audience, and communicative purpose, which is usually only with friends and at home in the case of Black Language. It promotes the use of one dialect, register, accent, or language variety over another, depending on social or cultural context, to project a specific identity. The end goal of this approach is to get Black students to use White Mainstream English. Anti-Black Linguistic Racism occurs when Black students are uncritically taught to code-switch without learning the social-cultural factors that inform the social positioning of Black Language and White Mainstream English.
	• **Contrastive Analysis**: an approach usually taught from a color-evasiveness perspective in conjunction with codes-switching. It teaches students about the differences and similarities between languages using the formality of the situation (i.e. use White Mainstream English in formal contexts and Black Language in formal contexts). Anti-Black Linguistic Racism is the assumption in this approach that Black Language does not have formal and informal registers. This approach creates a linguistic hierarchy that positions White Mainstream English as linguistically superior to Black Language and other linguistically marginalized languages.
Research/Disciplinary Discourse	• Research on Black Language that ignores the role that white linguistic hegemony, linguistic racism, and anti-blackness play in educational linguistic research.
	• Research on Black Language that does not examine Black Language as an embodied experience of blackness or divorces Black Language from its relationship to the Black experience and Black culture.
	• Research that ignores scholarship by Black Language scholars whose research agenda is also informed by their lived experiences as speakers of Black Language.

they imagined to be communicating in both languages. For the most part, the students drew images of Black people to reflect Black Language and white people to represent White Mainstream English. This is to be expected; however, what was troublesome was that the images and descriptions the students drew and wrote conveyed conceptions of blackness through the white imagination. For instance, most of the students described the speakers they drew to reflect Black Language as "bad," "ghetto," "thugs," and "trouble" all while describing White Mainstream speakers as "good," "proper," and "respectful." Fanon's (1952) theory of epidermalization suggests that Black children have been taught since early childhood to see themselves through the white imagination; that is, they have been unconsciously trained to correlate blackness with wrongness and whiteness with rightness.

Others have written about how Black students internalize Anti-Black Linguistic Racism and the impact it has on their language education and their linguistic, racial, and intellectual identities. In her article "Nobody means more to me than you and the future of Willie Jordan," Jordan (1988) describes a scenario where Black students in her undergraduate course, "In Search of the Invisible Black woman," reacted negatively to Alice Walker's written version of Black Language in her novel, *The Color Purple*. She states:

> Several students dumped on the book. Just about unanimously, their criticisms targeted the language. I listened to what they wanted to say and silently marveled at the similarities between their casual speech patterns and Alice Walker's written version of Black English. Here was a negative Black reaction to a prize-winning accomplishment of Black literature that White readers across the country had selected as a best seller. Black rejection was aimed at the one irreducibly Black element of Walker's work: the language—Celie's Black English.
>
> (Jordan, 1988, p. 125)

The students' reactions to Walker's use of Black Language in *The Color Purple* illustrates how deeply ingrained Anti-Black Linguistic Racism is in Black Language-speaking students. In this example, the students' internalization of Anti-Black Linguistic Racism contributed to their feelings of linguistic and cultural shame. According to Smitherman (1977), "an individual's language is intricately bound up with his or her sense of identity and group consciousness" (p. 171). All social groups want their group's identity to be positive; therefore, when an individual belongs to a group with a negative identification, their first impulse is to dissociate themselves from that group (Bedolla, 2003). Jordon argues that Black Language-speakers:

> either hide our original word habits, or we completely surrender our own voice, hoping to please those who will never respect anyone different from themselves: Black English is not exactly a linguistic buffalo, but we should understand its status as an endangered species, as a perishing, irreplaceable

system of community intelligence, or we should expect its extinction, and, along with that, the extinguishing of much that constitutes our own proud, and singular, identity.

(Jordan, 1988, p. 123)

Jordon's statement highlights the interconnection between Black Language and Black identity. Therefore, when Black students experience Anti-Black Linguistic Racism, it is not only an attempt to eradicate their group's language, it is also an attempt to eradicate their identity, community intelligence, theories of reality, and centuries of Black survival philosophies. In other words, to eradicate Black Language is to eradicate Black people's ways of knowing, interpreting, surviving, being, and resisting in the world.

In their 2008 study on language attitudes among Black boys, Kirkland and Jackson reveal how students in their mentoring program displayed internalized Anti-Black Linguistic Racism after engaging in contrastive analysis instruction. This was illustrated in the ways the students retained and sometimes reinforced negative attitudes about Black Language in and through the drawings they were asked to create to portray their language attitudes. Similar to the students at Leadership Academy, the boys in the mentoring program depicted Black Language-speakers with "criminal characteristics" and associated them with "violence," "drugs," and a "lack of education"; yet, they characterized White Mainstream English speakers as "successful," "accomplished," "calm," and wearing "suits and ties." Kirkland and Jackson (2008) concluded that:

> The students were, however, implicitly struggling with relationships between [Black Language] and [White Mainstream English] and the various and very different ways the languages constituted their identities. Although it was never explicitly dealt with in class, we noticed the students were struggling with how the languages positioned them in the world ...
>
> *(Kirkland & Jackson, 2008, p. 140)*

Kirkland and Jackson's study teaches us that any instruction that emphasizes the importance of White Mainstream English over all other linguistic forms is especially dangerous for Black students, and other linguistically marginalized students of color, as it communicates to them that being Black and speaking in Black Language are insufficient. One of the students in the study illustrates the consequences of these kinds of messages in his comment about language and success: "If I want to get a good job and be something in life, I gotta learn to talk White" (p. 142). The student's remark underscores Richardson's (2004) thinking that Black students are taught to hate their language which indirectly teaches them to hate themselves. The students in this study also illustrate the ways in which Black students are trained to view their language, identity, and culture through a white gaze in ways that negates their value, sense of self, and worth.

In a similar study, Kinloch (2010) examined two Black male students' perceptions of Black Language in their struggles to acquire academic success. The two undergraduate students in this study, Khaleeq and Phillip, are grappling with the idea of using White Mainstream English for academic success but also maintaining their identities as Black Language-speakers. Like the student in Kirkland and Jackson's (2008) study, Khaleeq and Phillip have internalized messages that suggest that they must speak White Mainstream English "to get a job," "become successful," "move up in the world, to not have to struggle as much, and to move out of [their] family's housing development unit and 'into a house'" (p. 120). Yet, they are struggling with how they can achieve this at the same time of maintaining their blackness. For instance, Kinloch (2010) states:

> As much as Phillip is aware of how he fixes his language, he is just as aware of the dilemma that such fixing involves. He battles with not wanting to fix his Black English because, he says, "that would mean something is wrong with me, yet … I want to be successful in life." His success, much like Khaleeq's, depends on not abandoning his cultural practices, language, and history of struggle. Nevertheless, he does not want to abandon the opportunities that can derive from knowing "standard English."
>
> *(Kinloch, 2010, p. 121)*

The language education that Phillip and Khaleeq received has caused them to develop what Smitherman refers to as linguistic push-pull—a linguistic interpretation of Dubois' theory of double consciousness. Smitherman coined the term linguistic push-pull in the 1970s to characterize the ambivalence Black Language-speakers feel about speaking Black Language; that is, "Black folk loving, embracing, using Black Talk, while simultaneously rejecting and hating on it" (Smitherman, 2006, p. 6). For Phillip and Khaleeq, their ambivalence comes from an anti-Black and culturally irrelevant language education that teaches them that they have to eradicate their culture and language to achieve upward mobility.

In her book *Vernacular Insurrections: Race, Black Protest, and the New Century in Composition-Literacies Studies*, Kynard (2013) includes a teaching interlude about one of her Black Language-speaking students, Sherrie, who was an outspoken advocate for speaking "proper English." In the interlude, Kynard shares how Sherrie had accepted a racialized linguistic inferiority or what I am referring to as internalized Anti-Black Linguistic Racism, in and through her writing.

> Sherrie would routinely do things in her weekly, informal journals assignments such as write two verb forms for the subjects of EACH of her sentences and circle one of them. The "answer" that she circled was usually "wrong." I had never seen anything like it: every noun had two verbs in parentheses, making her writing look like a handout from an elementary

school grammar workbook. When I asked Sherrie what all this circling was about, she told me that when she writes, she can't decide which verb form to choose so she puts both in brackets and goes back afterward to circle one.

(Kynard, 2013, p. 107)

As Kynard describes in her interlude, there are consequences for providing Black Language-speaking students like Sherrie with a language education that cuts them completely off from Black Language and offers a narrow view of White Mainstream English. In Sherrie's case, this form of Anti-Black Linguistic Racism had halted her writing and caused her to produce hypercorrection and experience writing anxiety that directly affected how she behaved in class (Charity Hudley & Mallinson, 2014). According to Charity Hudley and Mallinson (2014), hypercorrection occurs when speakers (or in Sherrie's case, writers) internalize the message that others view their language as wrong, therefore, they strive to use the standardized language so perfectly that they overarticulate in ways that miss the target of the perceived standard language in an effort to replace the seemingly incorrect language patterns (p. 64). Beyond the hypercorrection that she produced in her writing, Sherrie described her experiences in her English classes akin to child abuse: "You walk on eggshells, timid, and nervous, because any little mistake will set things off and get you punished" (Kynard, 2013, p. 108). Sherrie's comment speaks to how many Black Language-speaking students experience classrooms as violent and dehumanizing spaces and how our traditional language education perpetuates linguistic and racial violence.

As illustrated in each of the above examples, when Black students' language practices are suppressed or they begin to absorb anti-Black messages that imply that their language is deficient, wrong, or unintelligent, this can cause them to develop a linguistic double consciousness or negative attitudes about themselves and their linguistic, racial, cultural, and intellectual identities. South African linguist-revolutionary Neville Alexander said it best:

Being able to use the language(s) one has the best command of in any situation is an empowering factor and, conversely, not being able to do so is necessarily disempowering. The self-esteem, self-confidence, potential creativity and spontaneity that come with being able to use the language(s) that has or have shaped one from early childhood … is the foundation of all democratic politics and institutions. To be denied the use of these languages is the very meaning of oppression.

(qtd in Smitherman, 2017)

As Charity Hudley and Mallinson (2014) pointed out, this form of internalized racism can contribute to students losing "confidence in the learning process, their own abilities, their educators, and school in general" (p. 33).

Approaches to Language Education for Black Students: Toward an Antiracist Black Language Pedagogy

The Anti-Black Linguistic Racism that Black students experience and internalize when using Black Language in school is the product of their language education. Kynard (2013) argues that Black students learn to monitor their linguistic expressions based on how they have been treated and trained to view themselves in language arts classrooms (p. 109). Since the 1960s, language scholars have recognized that traditional ways of approaching language education in schools are anti-Black and uphold white linguistic hegemony. As argued by Labov (1970), deficit theories and pedagogies are extremely dangerous to the language education of Black students as they divert attention from the real defects of the educational system to imaginary defects of the child. In the section below, I describe two approaches that are commonly practiced in language arts classrooms: *eradicationist language pedagogies* and *respectability language pedagogies*. In contrast to these approaches, I offer *Antiracist Black Language Pedagogies* as a way forward.

Eradicationist Language Pedagogies

Teachers' failure to acknowledge the rich linguistic resources that Black students bring with them to classrooms has led to deficit approaches such as *eradicationist language pedagogies*, which work to eradicate Black Language from Black students' linguistic repertoires. Under this model, Black students' language practices are

TABLE 2.2 Approaches to Language Pedagogy

Eradicationist Language Pedagogies
Under this approach, Black Language is not acknowledged as a language and gets treated as linguistically, morally, and intellectually inferior. The goal of this approach is to eradicate Black Language from students' linguistic repertoires and replace it with White Mainstream English. Anti-Black Linguistic Racism is embedded in this approach as Black Language gets interpreted as a defect of the child rather than a defect of the educational system's response to it (Labov, 1970).

Respectability Language Pedagogies
Under this approach, Black Language is acknowledged as a language that should be validated, affirmed, and respected. However, the end goal of this approach is to simply use Black Language as a bridge to learn White Mainstream English. This approach perpetuates anti-blackness as it adheres to politics of respectability, surrenders to whiteness, and does not challenge Anti-Black Linguistic Racism.

Antiracist Black Language Pedagogy
Black Language is placed at the center of this approach to critically interrogate white linguistic hegemony and Anti-Black Linguistic Racism. The end goal of this approach is to dismantle Anti-Black Linguistic Racism and students' internalization of it, help Black students develop agency, take a critical stance, and make political choices (Kynard, 2007) that support them in employing Black Language "for the purposes of various sorts of freedom" (Richardson, 2004, p. 163).

viewed as deficient, and the goal is to correct what is presumed to be the deficiency and replace it with what is believed to be the better language, White Mainstream English (Paris, 2012). Anti-Black Linguistic Racism is embedded in eradicationist language pedagogies as these approaches deliberately deny Black students the right to use their native language as a linguistic resource during their language and literacy learning and attempts to annihilate Black linguistic and cultural norms. Smitherman (2017) reminds us that "when the language of instruction is not the student's home language, and students are silenced because they aren't allowed to use the language they know best, they are disadvantaged from the Git-Go" (p. 8). Though eradicationist approaches have been problematized in the scholarly literature, the students at Leadership Academy reminded me that this approach is still practiced in some language arts classrooms today.

Respectability Language Pedagogies

Recognizing the damage that deficit and eradicationist language pedagogies do to Black students, some language teachers and scholars turned to pedagogical approaches that seek to validate, affirm, and respect Black Language by using it as a bridge to teach White Mainstream English. I refer to these approaches as *respectability language pedagogies* (Baker-Bell, 2017). Building on Higginbotham's (1993) theory of "politics of respectability," respectability language pedagogies refer to approaches that view racially and linguistically marginalized students' language practices as valid and equal yet instruct these students to use White Mainstream English to avoid the negative stereotypes that are associated with their linguistic and racial backgrounds by appearing "respectable." Respectability pedagogies perpetuate anti-blackness as they do not fully accept or celebrate Black Language, and they teach Black students to respond to racism by adhering to white hegemonic standards of what it means to be "respectable" instead of teaching them to challenge, interrogate, and resist Anti-Black Linguistic Racism.

The most pervasive respectability language pedagogy that is used in language arts classrooms is the code-switching approach (Wheeler & Swords, 2006, 2010). As mentioned in Table 2.2, the code-switching approach requires racially and linguistically marginalized students to switch from the linguistic system of the language or dialect they are most familiar with to White Mainstream English. During classroom instruction, these students are taught to use language to fit the time, place, audience, and communicative purpose, and it promotes the use of one dialect, register, accent, or language variety over another, depending on social or cultural context, to project a specific identity. White Mainstream English tends to be promoted as the acceptable language to use most of the time, in most places, for most audiences, communicative purposes, and in most social and cultural contexts. I write more about code-switching and Black Language politics in chapter 4, but I want to briefly point out how code-switching pedagogies promote politics of respectability and uphold color-evasiveness[5] ideologies (Annamma, Jackson, & Morrison, 2017). This approach essentially posits that teachers should treat Black students' linguistic practices as equally as possible but should encourage them to code-switch to White Mainstream English to avoid discrimination. The problem with this approach, as applied in most classrooms, is that it encourages students to code-switch without any regard to their racial realities or the role that Anti-Black Linguistic Racism plays in why they are being asked to "code" their language in the first place. If our language arts instruction consisted of providing Black students with the critical linguistic tools to decode the notion of code-switching, they would find that this approach is asking them to do more than switch their language. Rather, they are being asked to switch their language, their cultural ways of being and knowing, their community, and their blackness in favor of a white middle class identity.

Still, some believe that Black students must code-switch to be successful in school and life. While I am not denying that some Black Language-speakers have not experienced temporary success by way of code-switching, I am questioning what gets lost or sacrificed in the process. What is really achieved? Who is privileged with making decisions about who has to code-switch to be successful and who does not? I have heard teachers use exceptionalism discourse with Black students by telling them that they can be the next "successful" or "rich" Black person (e.g. Barack Obama, Michelle Obama, Oprah, etc.) if they speak White Mainstream English. First of all, stop telling Black kids that they can be the next such and such and let them be the first version of themselves. Second, do we ever tell white students to code-switch so they can be the next Steve Jobs, Ellen DeGeneres, or Donald Trump? No, we do not! This is just downright racist. Also, stop playing like Oprah, Barack, Michelle, and nem don't speak Black Language. I have also heard teachers promise Black children that code-switching will help them get into college and earn a college degree. Ok! So give up your culture and your language in favor of achieving, at best, a house, a car, and a whole lot of college debt? Why would Black people want to give up parts of their identity and culture for this dull level of success? Everyone should be questioning this. My point is that we can't be out here using these mediocre and problematic measures of success that only legitimates a white status quo "American Dream, white picket fence" way of living that is tethered to the death of blackness and Black Language.

It is also important to interrogate code-switching in light of our current racial and political climate. In many classrooms, Black students are encouraged to code-switch as a strategy for survival; however, the students at Leadership Academy contested this belief. They questioned how code-switching to White Mainstream English could be a form of survival or self-protection when Black people are being discriminated against and killed based on the color of their skin (Baker-Bell, 2017). My work at Leadership Academy happened at the same time that George Zimmerman was on trial for the murder of Trayvon Martin. The students pointed out how Trayvon used White Mainstream English when he said "What are you following me for?" and that did not protect him from being murdered. The students' critical questioning of code-switching as a tool for survival in the face of racial violence cannot be ignored. There are indeed repetitive instances of Black people communicating in White Mainstream English and still having had acts of racial violence committed against them. I think about how code-switching or White Mainstream English did not protect Michael Brown who said, "I don't have a gun! Stop shooting!" before he was gunned down by police officer Darren Wilson. I think about Eric Garner who repeated the words "I cannot breathe" 11 times before he died after he was put in a chokehold by New York police officer Daniel Pantaleo. The students' thinking about Trayvon Martin also reminds me of Renisha McBride who communicated in White Mainstream English when she said "I just need to go home" to Theodore Wafer before he shot and killed her when she knocked on his door for help after getting into a car accident. I think about John Crawford who said "It is not real!" to police officers about an unpackaged BB/pellet air rifle he picked up and was holding in a Walmart store before police officers shot and killed him. I also think about Atatiana Jefferson, Aiyana Stanley-Jones, Tamir Rice, and countless other Black children and adults who were victims of racial violence before they could utter a word. These instances are clear reminders that code-switching into White Mainstream English will not save Black people and cannot solve racial or linguistic injustice, and we cannot pretend that it will.

The students at Leadership Academy compelled me to critically interrogate the relationship between language, racial violence, and language arts instruction: If using White Mainstream English cannot protect Black people from losing their lives, why are we telling Black children that code-switching is a strategy for survival? Black students understand that while they can switch their language, they cannot switch the color of their skin (Baker-Bell, 2017). At the end of the day, even if Black students choose to project a white middle class identity through language, it is nearly impossible for them to separate their language from their racial positioning in society (Flores & Rosa, 2015). We must be honest about this in our language instruction. We cannot continue to push respectability language pedagogies that require Black students to project a white middle class identity to avoid anti-blackness, especially when they are growing up amidst Black liberation movements like the Black Lives Matter movement, which stands against respectability politics and anti-blackness. To do so is essentially encouraging Black students to accept dominant narratives that help maintain "traditions of white privilege and Black oppression" (Richardson, 2004, p. 160).

Toward an Antiracist Black Language Education and Pedagogy

In contrast to language pedagogies and research that either attribute Anti-Black Linguistic Racism to presumed deficiencies of Black students' language practices, culture, behavior attitudes, families, or communities (King, 2005) or respond to Anti-Black Linguistic Racism by upholding white linguistic and cultural norms, I am forwarding Antiracist Black Language Pedagogy as a transformative approach to Black Language education. To be clear, a transformative approach to the language education of Black students cannot acquiesce to whiteness or side-step anti-blackness. These approaches are not transformative nor are they antiracist. Within an Antiracist Black Language education framework, I understand antiracism in terms of its relationship to challenging anti-blackness in theory, research, and practice. In particular, Nehrez's thinking about decolonization is important and necessary in making sense of what a transformative antiracist language education should entail:

> Decolonization ... continues to be an act of confrontation with a hegemonic system of thought; it is hence a process of considerable historical and cultural liberation. As such, decolonization becomes the contestation of all dominant forms and structures, whether they be linguistic, discursive, or ideological. Moreover, decolonization comes to be understood as an act of exorcism for both the colonized and the colonizer.
>
> *(qtd. in hooks, 1992, p. 1)*

In addition to Nehrez's wisdom, I want to underscore a salient point that Dumas and ross (2016) make in their theory of BlackCrit: "only a critical theorization of blackness confronts the specificity of anti-Blackness" (p. 416). As far as language education, this suggests that an Antiracist Black Language Pedagogy must (1) center blackness; (2) confront white linguistic and cultural hegemony; and (3) contest anti-blackness.

Though I am advocating for a transformative approach to Black Language education, I want to briefly situate my vision of Antiracist Black Language education within a larger context of radical Black intellectuals to illustrate how I am reclaiming and reconnecting with the ideas and recommendations that have already been put forth within the Black Language research tradition. Our ancestors and elders have always called out imperialist, racist, discriminatory approaches to language education that perpetuated Anti-Black Linguistic Racism and caused harm to Black students. Woodson (1933) is one of the earliest Black Language pioneers who interrogated the prevalence of anti-blackness in Black students' language education. He argued:

> In the study of language in school pupils were made to scoff at the Negro dialect as some peculiar possession of the Negro which they should despise rather than directed to study the background of this language as a broken-down African tongue—in short to understand their own linguistic history, which is certainly more important for them than the study of French Phonetics or Historical Spanish Grammar.
>
> *(Woodson, 1933, p. 10)*

Fanon (1952) examined the intersections between language, race, and culture and described how the hegemony embedded in this relationship produces an inferiority complex in Black people. He reminds us that "to speak a language is to appropriate its world and culture" (p. 21); thus, communicating in White Mainstream English is "appropriating the white world" (p. 19). Bailey (1968), who was the first Black woman linguist, argued that there was a need for drastic revisions in language arts curriculum. She called for instructional strategies that exploited the differences between Black Language and White Mainstream English. In 1981, Morrison called out how Black students are met with Anti-Black Linguistic Racism in schools:

> It is terrible to think that a child with five different present tenses comes to school to be faced with books that are less than his own language. And then to be told things about his language, which is him, that are sometimes permanently damaging ... This is a really cruel fallout with racism.
>
> *(qtd in Rickford & Rickford, 2000)*

Smitherman argued that "we have kids in the inner cities who are verbal geniuses, but we call them deficient in school and attempt to eradicate a part of their identity" (cited in Sealey-Ruiz, 2005). Building on Woodson's wisdom, Smitherman (2006) recommends that Black students' language education should consist of the study of "African American Language—its systematic properties, its history, the connection between AAL and African American life and culture" (p. 142).

Gilyard (1991) cautioned of the psychic costs Black students pay when acquiring White Mainstream English. He argued that "a pedagogy is only successful if it makes knowledge or skill achievable while at the same time allowing students to maintain their own sense of identity" (p. 11). Richardson (2004) pushed for an African American centered approach, which seeks to:

> explicate the production of African American knowledge or epistemology in order that we may develop appropriate language and literacy pedagogies to accelerate the literacy education of Black (and all) students ... in this way, then, African American centered education seeks to accelerate the learning of students of African descent by conscientizing them to their language, learning, and literacy traditions that are relevant to them, exploiting this knowledge in their acquisition of other discourses.
>
> *(Richardson, 2004, pp. 160–161)*

The abovementioned Black intellectuals make it clear that linguistic and racial justice for Black students are not rooted in anti-Black Language pedagogies that cater to whiteness, but in terms of the complete and total overthrow of racist, colonial practices so that antiracist language pedagogies might begin to be imagined, developed, and implemented. It is in this line of thinking that I imagine an

Antiracist Black Language education. In the section below, I outline ten framing ideas that are part of a broader educational movement that advocates for linguistic, racial, and educational justice for Black students.

Ten Framing Idea For an Antiracist Black Language Education and Pedagogy

1. critically interrogates white linguistic hegemony and Anti-Black Linguistic Racism.
2. names and works to dismantle the normalization of Anti-Black Linguistic Racism in our research, disciplinary discourses curriculum choices, pedagogical practices, and teacher attitudes.
3. intentionally and unapologetically places the linguistic, cultural, racial, intellectual, and self-confidence needs of Black students at the center of their language education.
4. is informed by the Black Language research tradition and is situated at the intersection of theory and practice.
5. rejects the myth that the same language (White Mainstream English) and language education that have been used to oppress Black students can empower them.
6. acknowledges that Black Language is connected to Black people's ways of knowing, interpreting, resisting, and surviving in the world (Richardson, 2004; Sanchez, 2007).
7. involves Black Linguistic Consciousness-raising that helps Black students heal and overcome internalized Anti-Black Linguistic Racism, develop agency, take a critical stance, and make political choices (Kynard, 2007) that support them in employing Black Language "for the purposes of various sorts of freedom" (Richardson, 2004, p. 163).
8. provides Black students with critical literacies and competencies to name, investigate, and dismantle white linguistic hegemony and Anti-Black Linguistic Racism.
9. conscientizes Black students the historical, cultural, political, and racial underpinnings of Black Language.
10. relies on Black Language oral and literary traditions to build Black students' linguistic flexibility and creativity skills. Provide students with opportunities to experiment, practice, and play with Black Language use, rhetoric, cadence, style, and inventiveness, which is necessary to use language effectively in a multilingual, multicultural world.

It is pivotal that the above ideas are embodied in any transformative approach that seeks to dismantle Anti-Black Linguistic Racism and students' internalization of it. In the next section, I briefly describe the praxis of these framing ideas by sharing seven Black Language Artifacts that emerged from the Antiracist Black Language Pedagogy that I used to engage students at Leadership Academy in critical conversations. The pedagogy consisted of several critical inquiry-based learning experiences that provided the students at Leadership Academy with an opportunity to learn Black Language, learn through Black Language, and learn about Black Language (Halliday, 1993) while simultaneously dismantling Anti-Black Linguistic Racism.

Antiracist Black Language Pedagogy

Black Language Artifact 1: Black Language & Identity

For this artifact, students examine the intersection of language, culture, and identity within the Black community.

Black Language Artifact 2: Language, History, & Culture

For this artifact, students will participate in a language study that examines the historical, cultural, and political underpinnings of Black Language.

Black Language Artifact 3: Study of the Grammatical and Rhetorical Features of Black Language Black Language

For this artifact, students will examine the structural and discourse features of Black Language.

Black Language Artifact 4: Language & Power

For this artifact, students will investigate the intersection of language and power.

Black Language Artifact 5: Language & Racial Positioning in Society

For this artifact, students examine the intersections between language and race. They will also be provided with opportunities to investigate the relationship between language and anti-blackness as one way of understanding linguistic racism.

Black Language Artifact 6: Language, Agency, & Action

For this artifact, students will develop agency, take a critical stance, and make political choices that support them in employing Black Language for the purposes of various sorts of freedom, including dismantling Anti-Black Linguistic Racism.

Black Language Artifact 7: Imagining a Language of Solidarity

For this artifact, students will develop a critical linguistic awareness and inter-rogate how other linguistically and racially diverse communities experience racial and linguistic violence and are impacted and are affected by linguistic racism.

I expand on these Black Language Artifacts in chapters 3 and 4, and I provide ethnographic snapshots that illustrate how the students at Leadership Academy engaged and interacted with each learning experience that these Black Language Artifacts provided. Some aspects of the artifacts were expanded, deepened, and redesigned following my research at Leadership Academy based on the lessons that I learned from the youth.

Notes

1 https://www.youtube.com/watch?v=MDM_6KZbrVg
2 https://www.ispot.tv/ad/ddJI/party-city-unicorn-party-song-by-dmx
3 http://www.mtv.com/news/2720889/teen-slang-2016/
4 Alim & Smitherman (2012) discuss this love-hate relationship on p. 25.
5 Following the work of Annamma, Jackson, and Morrison (2017), I use color-evasiveness in place of colorblindness. Color-evasiveness is a racial ideology that describes the act of denying the significance of race. Color-evasiveness also resists using colorblind ideologies because they position people with disabilities as problematic and use disabilities as a metaphor for weakness and limitations.

References

Alim, H. S., & Smitherman, G. (2012). *Articulate While Black: Barack Obama, Language, and Race in the U.S.* Oxford, NY: Oxford University Press.

Alim, H. S., Rickford, J. R., &Ball, A. (2016). *Raciolinguistics: How Language Shapes Our Ideas About Race.* New York, NY: Oxford University Press.

Annamma, S. A., Jackson, D. D., & Morrison, D. (2017) Conceptualizing color-evasiveness: using dis/ability critical race theory to expand a color-blind racial ideology in education and society. *Race Ethnicity and Education*, 2(20), 147–162.

Anzaldúa, G. (1987). *Borderlands: La frontera.* San Francisco, CA: Aunt Lute.

Bailey, B. (1968). Some aspects of the impact of linguistics on language teaching in disadvantaged communities. In A. L. Davis (Ed.), *On the Dialects of Children* (pp. 570–578). Champaign-Urbana, IL: National Council of Teachers of English.

Baker-Bell, A. (2017). "I can switch my language, but I can't switch my skin": What teachers must understand about linguistic racism. In E.Moore, Jr., A. Michael, & M. W. Penick-Parks (Eds.), *The Guide for White Women Who Teach Black boys* (pp. 97–107). Thousand Oaks, CA: Corwin Press.

Baker-Bell, A., Jones Stanbrough, R., & Everett, S. (2017). The stories they tell: Mainstream media, pedagogies of healing, and critical media literacy. *English Education*, 49(2), 130–152.

Baldwin, J. (1979, July 29). If Black English isn't a language, then tell me, what is? *New York Times.* Retrieved September 26, 2008, from www.nytimes.com

Baugh, J. (2000). *Beyond Ebonics: Linguistic Pride and Racial Prejudice.* Oxford, NY: Oxford University Press.

Baugh, J. (2015). Use and misuse of speech diagnostics for African American students. *International Multilingual Research Journal*, 9, 291–307.

Baugh, J. R., & King, S. (2016). Language and linguistics on trial: Hearing Rachel Jeantel (and other vernacular speakers) in courtroom and beyond. *Language*, 92(4), 944–988.

Bedolla, G. J. (2003). The identity paradox: Latino language, politics and selective dissociation. *Latino Studies*, 1(2), 264–283.

Bryan, N. (2020). Remembering Tamir Rice and other Black boy victims: Imagining Black PlayCrit literacies inside and outside of urban literacy education. *Urban Education*. Advance online publication: https://journals.sagepub.com/doi/full/10.1177/0042085920902250

Charity Hudley, M., & Mallinson, C. (2014). *We Do Language. English Language Variation in the Secondary English Classroom.* New York, NY: Teachers College Press.

Delgado, R., & Stefancic, J. (2017). *Critical Race Theory: An Introduction.* New York, NY: New York University Press.

Dumas, M., & ross, k. m. (2016). "Be real Black for me": Imagining blackcrit in education. *Urban Education*, 51(4), 415–442.

Dyson, M. E. (2009). A president-preacher from anaphora to epistrophe. *The Sydney Morning Herald.* Retrieved November 27, 2019, from https://www.smh.com.au/national/a-president-preacher-from-anaphora-to-epistrophe-20090119-gdta9b.html

Fanon, F. (1952). The Black Man and Language. In *Black Skin, White Masks.* New York: Grove Press.

Flores, N. & Rosa, J. (2015). Undoing appropriateness: Raciolinguistic ideologies and language diversity in education. *Harvard Educational Review*, 85(2), 149–171.

Gilyard, K. (1991). *Voices of the Self: A Study of Language Competence.* Detroit: Wayne State UP.

Higginbotham, B. E. (1993). Righteous discontent: The women's movement in the black Baptist church, 1880–1920. Cambridge: Harvard University Press.

Halliday, M. A. K. (1993). Towards a language-based theory of learning. *Linguistics and Education*, 5(2), 93–116.

hooks, b. (1992). Black looks: Race and representation. Boston, MA: South End Press.

hooks, b. (1994) Teaching to transgress: education as the practice of freedom. New York: Routledge.

Jeffries, M. (2014, November 28). Ferguson must force us to face anti-Blackness. Boston Globe. Retrieved from https://www.bostonglobe.com/opinion/2014/11/28/ferguson-must-force-face-anti-Blackness/pKVMpGxwUYpMDyHRWPln2M/story.html

Johnson, L. L. (2018). "Where do we go from here?": Toward a critical race English education. *Research in the Teaching of English*, 53, 104–124.

Johnson, L. L., Jackson, J., Stovall, D., & Baszile, D. T. (2017). "Loving Blackness to Death": (Re) Imagining ELA classrooms in a time of racial chaos. *English Journal*, 106(4), 60–66.

Jordan, J. (1988). Nobody mean more to me than you and the future life of Willie Jordan. *Moving Towards Home: Political Essays* (pp. 175–189). London: Virago.

King, E. J. (2005). *Black Education: A Transformative Research and Action Agenda for the New Century.* New York, NY: Routledge.

Kinloch, V. (2010). To not be a traitor of Black English: Youth perceptions of language rights in an urban context. *Teachers College Record*, 112(1), 103–141.

Kirkland, D. E., & Jackson, A. (2008). Beyond the silence: Instructional approaches and students' attitudes. In J. Scott, D. Y. Straker, & L. Katz (Eds.), *Affirming students' right to their own language: Bridging educational policies and language/language arts teaching practices* (pp. 160–180). Urbana, IL: NCTE/LEA.

Kynard, C. (2007). "I want to be African": In search of a Black radical tradition/African-American-Vernacularized Paradigm for "students' right to their own language. *College English*, 69, 360–390.

Kynard, C. (2013). *Vernacular Insurrections: Black Protest, and the New Century in Composition-Literacies Studies.* Albany, NY: SUNY Press.

Labov, W. (1970). The logic of non-standard English. In J. Alatis (Ed.), *Report of the Twentieth Annual Round Table Meeting on Linguistics Studies* (pp. 1–43). Washington, DC: Georgetown University Press.

Ladson-Billings, G., & Tate, W. F. (1995). Toward a critical race theory of education. *The Teachers College Record*, 97(1), 47–68.

Lippi-Green, R. (2012). *English with an Accent: Language, Ideology, and Discrimination in the United States*. New York, NY: Routledge.

Lorde, A. (1984). "The Master's Tools Will Never Dismantle the Master's House." *Sister Outsider: Essays and Speeches* (pp. 110–114). Berkeley, CA: Crossing Press.

Love, B. (2019). *We Want to Do More Than Survive: Abolitionist Teaching and the Pursuit of Educational Freedom*. Boston, MA: Beacon Press.

Paris, D. (2012). Culturally sustaining pedagogy: A needed change in stance, terminology, and practice. *Educational Researcher*, 41(3), 93–97.

Pimentel, C. (2011). The color of language: The racialized educational trajectory of an emerging bilingual student. *Journal of Latinos and Education*, 10(4), 335–353.

Richardson, E. (2004). Coming from the heart: African American students, literacy stories, and rhetorical education. In E. Richardson & R. Jackson (Eds.), *African American Rhetoric(s): Interdisciplinary Perspectives* (pp. 155–169). Carbondale, IL: Southern Illinois University Press.

Rickford, J. R., & Rickford, R. J. (2000). *Spoken Soul: The Story of Black English*. New York, NY: Wiley.

Sanchez, S. (2007). Sounds bouncin off paper: Black language memories and meditations. In S. Alim & J. Baugh (Eds.), *Talkin Black Talk: Language, Education and Social Change*. New York: Teachers College Press.

Sealey-Ruiz, Y. (2005). Spoken soul. The language of Black imagination and reality. *The Educational Forum*, 70, 37–46.

Smitherman, G. (1977). *Talkin and testifyin: The language of Black America*. Boston: Houghton Mifflin. (This version of the book is no longer available in print. The current version is published by Wayne State University Press.)

Smitherman, G. (2006). *Word from the Mother: Language and African Americans*. New York, NY: Routledge.

Smitherman, G. (2017). Raciolinguistics, "mis-education," and language arts teaching in the 21st century. *Language Arts Journal of Michigan*, 32(2), 4–12.

Stanford University. (2002). *Linguistics 73: How Linguists Approach the Study of Language and Dialect*. Stanford, CA: John Rickford.

Wheeler, R. S., & Swords, R. (2006). *Code Switching: Teaching Standard English in Urban Classrooms*. Urbana, IL: NCTE.

Wheeler, R. S., & Swords, R. (2010). *Code-Switching lessons: Grammar Strategies for Linguistically Diverse Writers*. Portsmouth, NH: firsthand Heinemann.

Wiley, T. G. (2000). Language planning and policy. In S.L. McKay & N.H. Hornberger (Eds.), *Sociolinguistics and Language Teaching* (pp. 103–147). Cambridge: Cambridge University Press.

Woodson, C. G. (1933). *The Mis-education of the Negro*. Washington, DC: Traffic Output Publication.

3

"KILLING THEM SOFTLY"

> When I came to school and was speaking like that when I was younger, all my teachers would tell me that's not the right way to talk. I just started crying...it took me down. I thought they were trying to scrutinize me!
>
> —*Janel, Leadership Academy*

I open up chapter 3 with these words from Janel because they shed light on how we are killing Black youth softly through anti-Black Language pedagogies. Her words underscore a point that Toni Morrison made in 1981:

> It is terrible to think that a child with five different present tenses comes to school to be faced with books that are less than his own language. And then to be told things about his language, which is him, that are sometimes permanently damaging ... This is a really cruel fallout with racism.
>
> *(Toni Morrison, qtd in Rickford & Rickford, 2000)*

As my responsibility to the Black students I have had the privilege of working with, I open chapter 3 by centering the voices and counterstories of the students at Leadership Academy. I am referring to their stories as counterstories because research, theories, and pedagogies on Black Language education are not very inclusive of Black students' perspectives about their language learning or everyday language experiences. Smitherman (1998) reminds us that "language is critical in talking about the education of a people because it represents a people's theory of reality; it explains, interprets, constructs, and reproduces that reality" (p. 154). By listening to their stories in my own research, I was able to see how their experiences with language counter the dominant story about Black Language and what Black students need in a language education. Their counterstories affirm that eradicationist and respectability approaches to Black Language education do not account for the emotional harm, internalized Anti-Black Linguistic Racism, or consequences these approaches have on Black students' sense of self and identity. Their voices and stories matter! And as educators and researchers, we must listen and engage their perspectives in our research, theories about language learning, and pedagogical practices. The questions I ask readers to consider while reading this chapter are: What stories do Black students tell about their experiences with the language education they are offered in school? How are Black students impacted by Anti-Black Linguistic Racism?

My First Read of Leadership Academy

I started my project at Leadership Academy (hereafter LA), a public charter school located on Detroit's Westside, in the spring of 2013. Though I was born, reared, and raised on the Westside of Detroit, I was not too familiar with LA because it had been open for only two years when I began my work there. I learned about the school through Ms. Helen, a teacher at LA who I met when I began my teaching career back in 2003. Ms. Helen and I go way back—she participated in many of my previous Black Language Pedagogy research projects. LA served approximately 200 ninth and tenth grade students, and ninety-nine percent of the students who attended were Black American. More than half of the teachers who taught at LA were white. All of the classes at LA were gender-based, including the two ninth grade ELA classes I worked in. LA had a strong focus on preparing their students to be scholars and leaders who would achieve at the rigorous level necessary to ultimately graduate with a college degree and thrive in life. As I began learning more about LA, I could not help but give it the side-eye. The gender-based classrooms rubbed me the wrong way because they are not inclusive of transgender and gender non-binary students, and they reinforce gender binaries and cisheteronormativity. I also did not care for LA's very strict dress code policy and uniform expectations because they perpetuated anti-blackness. For example, the students were prohibited from rocking head scarves, hoodies, or haircuts with designs—all Black cultural styles and fashions. The schools' strict and oppressive uniform policies and gender-based classrooms suggested that the students' gender and cultural freedoms and identities were being vilified, policed, and seen as antithetical to learning and success.

When I arrived at the school on the first day that my project began, something felt very familiar about the school. Perhaps it was the brown two-story brick building with a few portable classrooms located on the playground, indicating that the school was overcrowded, that was reminiscent of some of the elementary and middle schools I attended in Detroit in the 80s and early 90s. Maybe it was the heavy, metal double doors or the metal detectors that reminded me of some of the high schools I taught at in the city. Once I made it past the metal detectors, the walls greeted me with beautiful mural paintings of Black students that communicated "Black academic excellence." I also noticed a painting of the school's logo and mission statement on one of the walls. To get to Ms. Helen's classroom, I walked past a line of tan lockers, and I took a flight of stairs to arrive on the second floor. I noticed that a few of the steps were cracked and stained, which was a strong indicator that LA had purchased a vacant school building but did minimum renovations—a common narrative among Detroit charter schools. I opened one of the double doors to enter the second floor and I noticed two students walking down the hall wearing the school's uniform (khaki pants and navy-blue shirts), and I heard a few voices in the teachers' lounge that was located across from Ms. Helen's classroom. I entered Ms. Helen's room, and we greeted each other with a hug. She did not have any students in her class at the time because her second hour was her prep. As I chatted with Ms. Helen, I looked around the room at the desks that formed a Socratic circle. I noticed a Do Now prompt on the board that asked students to write about violence and video games. Next to the Do Now was a screen that was connected to a projector. In the corner of the room was an outdated TV and VCR attached to the wall that looked like they had not been used in decades. The wall in the back of the room was decorated with student work. The room was well-lit and had multiple windows that provided a view of the neighborhood that surrounded the school: brick ranch style houses, green grass, colorful flowers, and a few cars parked in front of some of the houses.

"What They Call You Where You From?" Separating the Real from the Fake

The bell rang, and students began trickling into the classroom one at a time. A few of the students noticed me sitting in a desk in one of the corners of the room. One of the students waved, and I waved back. Another student looked at me from head to toe. His eyes seemed to ask, "who are you and what are you doing in my class?" A student, who I would later come to know as B.O.B., asked Ms. Helen: "Who is dat, Ms. H?" Ms. Helen introduced me to the students by saying:

> Remember I told you all about Ms. Baker-Bell? She's here from Michigan State University and will be working with us for a few months on a project about language. She's not like those other people—you know the ones that I'm talking about. They come watch us and then we never see them again. Ms. Baker-Bell is not like that; she's good!

The "other people" that Ms. Helen was referring to are the "hit it and quit it" researchers that enter into schools and classrooms, collect data, and bounce. Researchers have hit and quit LA so much that even the students had their own vetting process for determining who were legit researchers and who were not. For example, a few days after coming to the school, some of the students asked Ms. Helen if they could ask me a few questions because *they needed answers*.

"Ms. Baker-Bell, Did you grow up in the D?" Janel asked.

"Yep, I sure did," I responded.

"Eastside or Westside?" Chasse followed up.

"Westside! Fenkell and Southfield." I replied.

"What high school did you attend?" Lola asked.

"Redford" I said. I was wondering if they had heard of the school because it had been closed for nearly a decade.

"Dang, that school ain't even open no more. My aunty went there too." Allistar responded.

We all laughed.

"Okay! Okay! You said you was a teacher in Detroit too, right? Which schools did you teach at?" Fetti asked.

"I taught at DAAS, Crockett, and DIA," I answered.

"How old are you? You got any kids?" Janel asked.

"Yeah, I got two kids. And, how old do I look?" I chuckled.

"Can you tell us what this is going to be about?" B.O.B. questioned.

"Overall, I want to learn about your experiences using language at school and in the world. I am hoping that my learning from y'all will help me and other teachers become better at our jobs," I added.

The students' series of questions are reflective of what I would call a Detroit literacy practice. That is, when Detroiters meet other Detroiters, they ask a series of questions that helps them to place each other geographically on a map and/or distinguish *the real* (those who live/lived in Detroit) from *the fake* (those who claim Detroit but have never lived there or did not live there pregentrification).

Black Language Artifact 1: Black Language & Identity

The first Black Language Artifact (Figure 3.1) was designed to initiate a conversation about Black Language and White Mainstream English at the same time of unveiling the students' initial attitudes toward both languages. The activity, which I refer to as an attitudinal assessment, asked the students to: (1) read two language samples,[1] (2) draw an image, cartoon, or character that reflects each language sample, and (3) write a paragraph that expressed their thoughts about both languages and the speakers of those languages. At that time, the students were not aware that *language sample A* represented features of Black Language and *language sample B* represented features of White Mainstream English. This move was intentional as I did not want the students to become distracted or influenced by the labels used to identify the language variations this early in the study, but instead, my purpose was to capture their language attitudes and reveal how they were impacted by Anti-Black Linguistic Racism before and after

I implemented the Black Linguistic Consciousness-raising component of the Antiracist Black Language Pedagogy.

Inspired by Kirkland and Jackson's (2008) study on Black students' language attitudes, I used the following Black Language Artifact as a pre- and post-activity to help determine whether or not the Antiracist Black Language Pedagogy could interrupt the students' internalization of Anti-Black Linguistic Racism.

Albeit straightforward, the attitudinal assessment activity provided deep insight into the ways the students navigated and negotiated Anti-Black Linguistic Racism. Additionally, as I will illustrate later in this chapter, inviting the students to draw images to represent the language samples helped me get underneath their language attitudes where their perceptions of their cultural, racial, and intellectual identities in the face of anti-blackness and white linguistic and cultural hegemony were buried. Drawings, like other visual texts, can reveal additional information about youth and children's beliefs, values, and perceptions that may not get captured through written or oral communication (Albers, Holbrook, & Flint, 2013). For instance, Kirkland and Jackson (2008) found that having their students create drawings afforded them an opportunity to represent visually how "attitudes about language speak back to selves and societies" (p. 142). I asked the students at LA to work individually on the attitudinal assessment before I invited them to participate in a group dialogue about their responses to the activity. I offer a composite counterstory of that dialogue, which highlights how deeply ingrained Anti-Black Linguistic Racism is in our education system and in the minds of many Black

Language A:	Language B:
• People be thinkin' teenagers don't know nothin'.	• Teenagers know more than people think they do.
• We be talking about current events all the time in our history class.	• We discuss current events in our history class on a regular basis.
• Yesterday, we was conversating with Mr. B. about the war--it was deep.	• Yesterday, we were having a conversation with our teacher about the war--it was a rich conversation.
• The teachers at South High is cool.	
• But Ms. Nicks do be trippin' sometimes. Like that time she got really mad because Rob called her a dime piece.	• The teachers at South high school are cool.
• Ms. Nicks better quit trippin' or imma drop her class like it's hot.	• However, my cousin thinks the students at South high are disrespectful.
• My cousin think the students at South High are all mean and stuff.	• I informed her that she was mistaken. Not all of the students are disrespectful.
• The students ain't as bad as she think though.	
• I told her she wrong about that.	

FIGURE 3.1 Attitudinal Assessment

students. Before presenting the dialogue, I want to briefly discuss why I chose to use composite character counterstorytelling to recount the students' experiences and attitudes about language.

Composite Character Counterstorytelling

Composite character counterstorytelling is a critical race methodological tool that allows researchers to merge data analysis with creative writing to expose patterns of racialized inequality and deepen our understanding of the ways race and racism affects the lives and lived experiences of people of color as individuals and as groups in schools (Cook, 2013). This method is used to counter majoritarian myths and narratives that get perpetuated about linguistically and racially diverse groups in education. Many researchers who use this method analyze the data and create a story involving composites and fictional characters. According to Solorzano and Yosso (2002), composite character counterstories are not simply fictionalized narratives and imaginary characters drawn from data; instead they are grounded in real-life experiences and actual empirical data and are contextualized social situations that are also grounded in real life, not fiction (p. 36).

I used composite character counterstorytelling as a mechanism to represent both complexity and simplicity in interpreting and presenting the central ideas gleaned from the rich and multifaceted data gathered in this study. In particular, composite character counterstorytelling provided me with a method for weaving together the interview transcripts, field notes, research memos, artifacts, and other research data into a coherent narrative that captured and provided a thorough depiction of how the students at LA understood their linguistic realities. To be clear, the events that I describe throughout this book, such as the dialogue I write about below, did actually occur. However, because the study took place across two classrooms, the use of composite character counterstorytelling created space for me to bring together data from both classes to present a collective portrayal that more fully speaks to the cumulative impact of Anti-Black Linguistic Racism and "draw attention to how individual experiences are representative of collective experiences within racial structures" (Cook, 2013, pp. 190–191).

Within this collective portrayal, I created composite characters by representing multiple students at LA as a single character to capture richer, more detailed and robust stories of the students' language attitudes and relationship with Anti-Black Linguistic Racism. Before constructing the composite characters, I analyzed the data and wrote the narratives of each student involved in the study to capture the essence of each individual. I then used the following three themes that emerged from the data regarding students' language attitudes and their relationship with Anti-Black Linguistic Racism to construct the composite characters: *internalized Anti-Black Linguistic Racism, linguistic double consciousness,* and *Black Linguistic Consciousness*. I return to these concepts along with an analysis of how they were reflected in the students' language attitudes later in this chapter. In addition to their language attitudes, I constructed the composite characters using aspects of their language use, body language, personalities, perspectives, histories, and language experiences. Again, the composite character counterstories emanate from data collected from multiple students who participated in the study. The counterstories that I present throughout the remainder of this book are reflective of the sentiments, words, and stories the students at LA shared.

Group Dialogue: So What Y'all Think?

"Okay, so let's talk about what y'all wrote for both language samples," Ms. Baker-Bell said as she sketched a perpendicular line on the dry erase board to imitate the pre-attitudinal assessment. "Let's begin with language sample A—what did you write?"

"It's slang and incorrect," Janel blurted.

Her response was immediately followed by B.O.B.'s comment, "Yep, I said the same thang! Slang and ghetto!"

As Ms. Baker-Bell hurriedly wrote Janel and B.O.B.'s responses on the dry erase board (Figure 3.3)., the comments from other students came quickly:

"Trouble"
　"Bad kids"
　"Sloppy"
　"Loud"
　"From the inner-city"
　"Alright then. What did y'all think about language sample B?" Baker-Bell queried as she continued to scribble their responses on the board.

"I said it's a person who is respectful, loves school, and is always ready and prepared," Lola commented.

"Umm hmm. I put proper and knowledgeable," Janel added.

"I imagined it to be someone from the suburbs," a voice from the back of the room added to the conversation.

"Alright! I got it! Now, who's interested in sharing with me the image they drew for each language sample and why?" Ms. Baker-Bell asked.

Allistar looked around the classroom at the other students to see if anyone would respond before he did. "I'll go," he said in a nonchalant manner.

"For language A [Black Language], I said I think this is someone with little education or someone who is just trying to be cool. He has his beater on and sagging pants. Maybe it is what he like or even all he know. I think he knows better but just don't do it. He looks like a thug because he look like he does not care. He have no car but nice clothes, and he loves to talk about others."

"And, for language B [White Mainstream English]," Allistar continued, "I wrote that I think this guy went to college and have a interview. He is very smart and or is trying to fit in. He has a house and a car and is striving for the best."

Allistar then stood up to show everyone the images he drew to represent both language samples. I could hear some of the students laughing as he waved his drawing around for everyone to see (Figure 3.2)

Responding to the striking resemblance between Allistar and the character he drew to represent someone who would communicate in Black Language, Fetti Bravo, who was sitting next to Allistar, blurted out, "ole boy under language A look just like you, man."

Before Allistar could respond to Fetti, Chase interrupted with "Okay, okay. Let me go. It's my turn. For person A, I drew an African American who sags & wears their hat backwards. And drawing B is a white person who wears belts and their hats on straight."

"I think language A is somebody who dresses like a thug and runs the streets," B.O.B. shouted.

Lola, added, "Yeah, for character A, I drew like bad kids. Like they don't care about school…"

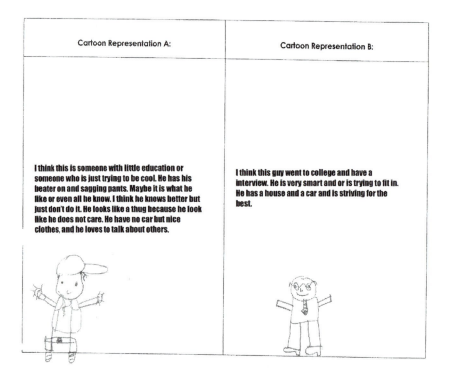

FIGURE 3.2 Allistar's Drawing for Attitudinal Assessment

Janel quickly interjected: "But that's not true. Just because you talk with slang don't mean you don't care about school."

"I'm not saying it's everybody, but certain people do think like that," Lola replied.

(Silence fills the classroom.)

"I'm just listening to this whole conversation and shaking my head. We can't assume because a person speaks a certain way that they are automatically bad," Fetti Bravo commented.

What immediately stands out from the group dialogue is that many of the students' drawings, comments, and perspectives reinscribe a linguistic and racial hierarchy that positions Black Language and blackness as inferior and White Mainstream English and whiteness as superior, thus reinscribing and reinforcing whiteness and anti-blackness. For instance, "smart" and "good" became synonymous with white linguistic and

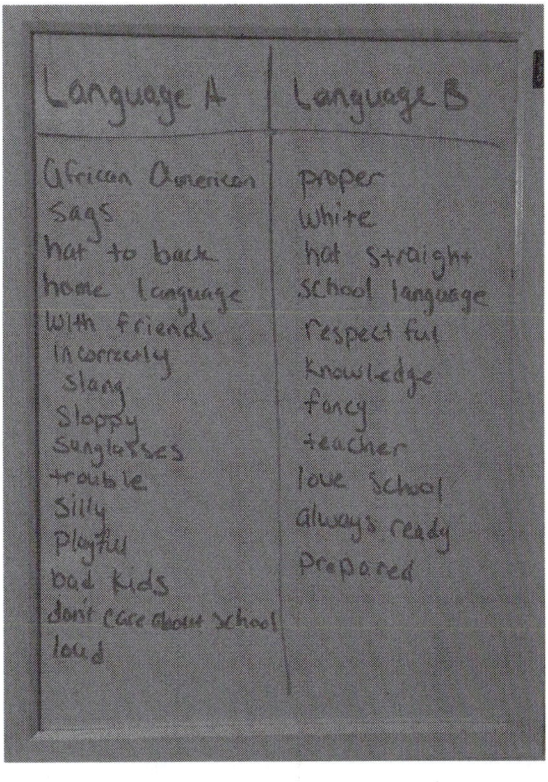

FIGURE 3.3 Responses Collected in Dry Erase Board

cultural norms, yet the students conflated words and images such as "disrespectful," "thug," "ghetto," "bad," "trouble," "skips school," and "gets bad grades" with Black linguistic and cultural norms. As difficult as it was for me to listen to Black students reinforce anti-blackness and Anti-Black Linguistic Racism, their perspectives are to be expected according to hooks (1992) who argues that Black people are socialized within a white supremacist society, white supremacist educational system, and racist mass media that teach us to internalize racism by convincing us that our lives (culture, language, literacies histories, experiences, etc.) are not complex and are unworthy of sophisticated critical analysis and reflection (hooks, 1992, pp. 1–2). This oftentimes leads to Black people unconsciously and sometimes consciously constructing images of ourselves through the lens of white supremacy (hooks, 1992, pp. 1–2). In this way, the students' responses to the attitudinal assessment mirror the ways in which they have been socialized to understand their linguistic, cultural, and racial identities in and through their language education and society.

Although the group dialogue suggests that many of the students did internalize Anti-Black Linguistic Racism, it also shows that some of the students were beginning to engage in a form of dialogic consciousness-raising (Paris, 2011; Baker-Bell, Paris, & Jackson, 2017). We see this with Janel and Fetti Bravo, who push back on their classmate's assumptions about people who communicate in Black Language. Janel argues that "just because you talk with *slang* don't mean you don't care about school" while Fetti Bravo insists that "we can't assume because a person speaks a certain way that they are automatically bad." The students' responses during the dialogue are telling of why Black students need an Antiracist Black Language Pedagogy that provides them with "alternative ways to look at blackness, black subjectivity, and, of necessity, whiteness" (hooks, 1992, p. 5).

The Impact of Anti-Black Linguistic Racism

Following the group dialogue, I met with a few of the students individually to have a more in-depth conversation with regard to their thinking about Black Language and White Mainstream English. The conversation, along with their responses to the attitudinal assessment and group dialogue, helped me to make sense of their language attitudes and how they were individually and collectively impacted by Anti-Black Linguistic Racism before I implemented the Black Linguistic Consciousness-raising component of the Antiracist Black Language Pedagogy. Their responses suggested a complex and nuanced relationship with Anti-Black Linguistic Racism. I use the following three descriptors to capture the complexity and the variations I observed in their responses throughout the study: *internalized Anti-Black Linguistic Racism, linguistic double consciousness*, and *Black Linguistic Consciousness*. I am using the descriptor internalized Anti-Black Linguistic Racism to describe the students' responses that indicated they unconsciously supported white linguistic hegemony and perpetuated anti-blackness and Anti-Black

Linguistic Racism. Linguistic double consciousness describes the students whose responses reflected their linguistic ambivalence. That is, their responses suggested that they both resisted and perpetuated Anti-Black Linguistic Racism and white linguistic and cultural hegemony. Finally, I use the descriptor Black Linguistic Consciousness to characterize the students whose responses illustrated how they critically interrogated and consistently resisted white linguistic hegemony and Anti-Black Linguistic Racism. Though I am describing Black Linguistic Consciousness in this chapter, I did not observe this perspective in any of the students' responses until after I implemented the consciousness-raising component of the Antiracist Black Language Pedagogy (more on this in chapter 5). In fact, my analyses showed that out of the 16 students who participated in the study from the beginning to the end, 14 of their responses to the attitudinal assessment and dialogue reflected Anti-Black Linguistic Racism and two of their responses reflected linguistic double consciousness before I implemented the consciousness-raising component of the Antiracist Black Language Pedagogy.

While these descriptors are useful in describing the variation, nuances, and complexities in the students' language attitudes and the ways they are impacted by the Anti-Black Linguistic Racism they experience in school and in their everyday lives, it is important to note that their attitudes and perspectives may have also been influenced by the study taking place in the context of school—a space they associate with an "assimilationist and often violent white imperial project [that requires them] to lose or deny their languages, literacies, cultures, and histories in order to achieve in schools" (Paris & Alim, 2017, p. 1). Indeed, some of the students could have been so acclimated to "performing school" and not having their voices heard, that some of their responses to the early activities within the Antiracist Black Language Pedagogy could mirror the broader language attitudes and Anti-Black Linguistic Racism that are perpetuated in schools rather than a full reflection of their own attitudes and beliefs. In the remaining sections of this chapter, I offer two composite character counterstories that illustrate the two dominant variations I noticed in the students' responses: internalized Anti-Black Linguistic Racism and linguistic double consciousness. These composite character counterstories capture the students' relationship with Anti-Black Linguistic Racism before I implemented the consciousness-raising component of the Antiracist Black Language Pedagogy.

A Composite Character Counterstory about Janel's Linguistic Double Consciousness

> "Girl, I be wearing my brother's basketball shorts and stuff," Janel said to Lola as they walked through the doors of Leadership Academy a few minutes before the first bell rang.
> Lola looked at Janel with a side-eye and replied, "That's ghetto."

"I don't care," Janel replied and shrugged her shoulders as she entered the combination to the locker that her and Lola shared.

"Do we need our ELA books for Ms. Helen's class today?" Janel asked Lola.

"Nah, I don't think so! I think that lady from MSU is going to be here today—what's her name?"

"Oh, that's right. Her name is Ms. Baker-Bell! " Janel quickly responded.

Lola and Janel hung their coats in the locker and began walking to class. The girls wore navy blue vests, white shirts, light-khaki colored dress pants, black belts, and black dress shoes—a required uniform at LA. Like many of the students, Janel and Lola's uniforms followed the school's dress code to a tee, but their Ebonics violated what some of their teachers deemed *the language of school*. When they turned the corner, their classmate, Allistar, ran past them, nearly knocking Janel's folder out of her hand.

"Little boy! If you don't slow your roll! You ain't bout to make it to class on time no way," Janel yelled.

"My bad, J! You know I cain't be late for Ms. Helen's class no more," Allistar responded as he continued running down the hall.

"Who is that speaking like they don't know proper English," Ms. Lockett said to Ms. French. When Ms. Lockett turned around and saw that it was Janel, her frown turned into a half-smile. She shook her head and said, "Now I know you know better. Your PSAT scores are too high for you to be speaking like you lack intelligence, young lady." Ms. Lockett was the principal at LA, and Ms. French was Janel's math teacher.

Janel, who called herself the queen of code-switching, smirked and said, "sorry, Ms. Lockett."

"Ummm hmmm," Ms. Lockett responded sarcastically.

As Janel and Lola walked up the stairs toward Ms. Helen's classroom, Janel said "You see how quick Ms. Lockett switched her attitude when she saw it was me speaking in slang?"

"Right! If that was anybody else, she would have went in on them," Lola replied as she shook her head.

"Fasho, girl! It's these high PSAT scores. They know I'm smart! I could sit here and talk like this for days, but if I'm getting my work done, I'm getting my work done," Janel firmly stated.

Janel and Lola walked into Ms. Helen's class and took their seats as the bell rang. A few minutes later, Allistar walked into the room sweating profusely. Janel looked at Allistar and said, "I told you! I knew you wasn't going to be on time."

Janel then glanced at the two language samples on the sheet that Ms. Baker-Bell asked her and the other students to complete. "*People be thinkin' teenagers don't know nothin"* Janel silently read to herself. *Hmmm. This is how me and my friends talk. We can all relate to this language,* Janel thought as she continued to ponder on the language samples. *Yeah, I'd definitely use this language with my friends because if I spoke in language B around them, they would ask me why I'm talking like that or they'd think I'm trying to be smarter than them or something. On the other hand, I would speak like language B when I'm around an administrator or teacher,* Janel thought as she reminded herself of the interaction she had with Ms. Lockett before class. *Okay, so I am going to draw a picture and write a response that show how these languages represent two sides of me.*

Janel drew her picture (Figure 3.4) and wrote the following response on the attitudinal assessment: The difference between language A and language B is: language A is used when I am with my friends, and I am comfortable enough to talk in "slang" or incorrectly. In language B, I don't want to seem unintelligent or ignorant, so I talk properly or knowledgeably in front of an administrator.

After Janel, Lola, and Allistar left Ms. Helen's class that day, they continued to talk about the activity and dialogue they had with Ms. Baker-Bell. During lunch, they reminisced about their experiences using Black Language.

FIGURE 3.4 Janel's Drawing on Attitudinal Assessment

"But forreal ... that activity really got me thinking about what's considered incorrect or slang," Janel said as she paid for her lunch. "Because when you're taught language, you're just taught a certain way to say things ... and if you change it up, then it's incorrect. Like if I put *ain't* on a sentence test, they gonna say that's wrong, but if I say *am not*, then that's right so ..."

"You ain't never lied," Lola responded as she threw her hands in the air to suggest she gives up.

"But if I say *ain't* to my friends, then *ain't* is right and *am not* is wrong," Janel added. Allistar nodded in agreement.

As the trio sat down at the lunch table, Janel reminded them of the language policing that happens in their math class. "Y'all know Ms. French will correct us too quick," Janel said as she opened up her bag of chips. Lola and Allistar laughed as Janel began imitating Ms. French.

"She be like 'that's not the right way.' And the students be like 'we not in English—this math class, Ms. French.'"

"Yep!" Allistar grinned. "Do y'all remember that time when I said the answer to the math problem was *one-o-fo*, and she made me repeat the whole sentence as if *one-o-fo* and one hundred and four don't mean the same thang?"

"I remember that," Lola nodded and shook her head. "So unnecessary."

"And truth be told ...", Janel said, "Ms. Helen be correcting us all the time, but some of the other teachers don't care as long as we getting our work done."

"Nope, Ms. Helen don't like us using choppy sentences either," Allistar responded.

"Umm Hmm," Lola interjected to express agreement with Janel and Allistar.

"But real talk ... when I came to school and I was speaking like that when I was younger, all of my teachers would tell me 'that's not the right way to talk' or they'd say I was speaking wrong. That made me feel sad, and I would just start crying. I thought they were trying to scrutinize me," Janel shared.

"Dang, J! That's sad!" Allistar responded.

"It really is! Even sadder that it happened at church too," Janel said in a very serious, but frustrating tone. "When I used to go to church, there were a whole bunch of boujee people who was like from 21 mile. They was like, 'she ghetto. She don't know nothing. She just gonna be a rat or turn out to be a baby momma' ... they were being so judgmental. In church, though!? In church!"

"Because of the way you talk?" Lola asked.

"... because of the way I talk" Janel quickly responded. "They didn't know nothing about me. They didn't know if I went to school. All these As and Bs I get in school, and they just assumed that I'm just unintelligent or I could be a baby momma or didn't do none of my work. They don't even know me," Janel said with frustration in her voice.

"Sometimes I feel like that when my parents correct me," Allistar said.

"Oh my god! If I'm with my momma, she'll correct me too, but if I'm with my daddy, he be talking the same way with me ... he be like 'girl, you betta come on,' but that's only when he talking to us [Janel and her siblings]. When he talk on the phone, he be talking correct like 'hello,'" Janel said in a way to mimic white middle class ways of speaking. "I be like you ain't slick, daddy!"

Lola and Allistar started cracking up. Janel joined them in the laughter.

"But forreal ... if I'm in my house, then I'm gonna talk how I feel like talking and that's probably going to be slang because it's easier. It's not like I gotta pronounce all those words. I just say what I feel like saying," Janel continued. "At the end of the day, I think it is more smart for you to talk in both languages rather than speak in one language or talk proper all the time. If you can do both, then it show that you are obviously smart."

The bell rang and Janel, Lola, and Allistar left the lunch room and walked to Ms. French's class.

Reflecting on Janel's Linguistic Double Consciousness:

In the composite character counterstory about Janel's linguistic double consciousness, we are able to observe the ways in which she navigates and negotiates her linguistic identity across various situations. Her language experiences have contributed to her feeling conflicted and ambivalent toward Black Language. In one way, Janel embraced Black Language and felt compelled to defend its honor, yet there are moments where she acquiesces to politics of respectability and perpetuates Anti-Black Linguistic Racism. As noted in the counterstory, Janel continuously resisted and pushed back on Anti-Black Linguistic Racism. For instance, she challenges the dominant narrative which suggests that a person who communicates in Black Language is academically inferior by pointing out her high PSAT score and superior grades in school. By highlighting her academic achievements while simultaneously admitting to being a speaker of Black Language, Janel is disrupting "interpretations of Black linguistic forms as signs of Black intellectual inferiority and moral failings" (Alim & Smitherman, 2012, p. 24). She also confronts the antiblackness embedded in monolingual ideologies when she states, "it is more smart for you to talk in both languages rather than speak in one language." In other words, Janel is suggesting that bilingual Black Language-speakers are not linguistically inferior to monolingual White Mainstream English-speakers. Janel's thinking is in line with Alim and Smitherman's (2012) argument about the cultural-linguistic hegemony that "imposes itself on people, and praises them for 'covering up' their own language varieties rather than rewarding them for speaking multiple language varieties" (p. 48).

The composite character counterstory also reveals how Janel and her peers developed creative ways to resist Anti-Black Linguistic Racism. We see this in the scenario that Janel, Lola, and Allistar described from their math class. In response to Ms. French's language policing, the students suggested that they would use humor to remind Ms. French that she teaches math, not English. Essentially, the students are trying to help Ms. French understand that their linguistic background should not interfere with their ability to learn. We also see Janel use creative resistance in how she navigated and negotiated the language policing that Ms. Lockett subjected her to. Although Janel smirks and apologizes to Ms. Lockett for using Black Language instead of White Mainstream English, in her conversation with Lola, she points out the irony in Ms. Lockett's response. That is, Ms. Lockett affirms Janel's intelligence at the same time of checking her for not sounding intelligent. Janel also tells Lola that while she's able to use her grades and PSAT scores as a shield to protect her from being chastised by Ms. Lockett, this is not the case for other students whose intelligences may not be expressed academically or may get overlooked in school spaces.

While Janel's counterstory illustrates that she found creative ways to resist the Anti-Black Linguistic Racism she endured in school and in everyday life, it also shows how she sometimes internalized and perpetuated anti-Black messages about her language. This is exemplified by her description of Black Language and Black Language-speakers as "incorrect," "unintelligent," "ignorant," and "does not appear knowledgeable." These terms are informed by a white supremacist ideological lens that interprets Black Language as a symbol of intellectual and moral inferiority and reflects racist beliefs about Black people. Janel also illustrates that she has internalized Anti-Black Linguistic Racism in her rationale of how she navigates and negotiates language. In her written response, Janel states that she uses Black Language when she is with her friends because she feels comfortable speaking in "slang or incorrectly," and she explains that she will use White Mainstream English when she does not want people, specifically authority figures, to view her as unintelligent or ignorant. As Smitherman (1977) pointed out decades ago, this perspective is often upheld by members of the Black speech community, and it suggests that Janel, like many Black Language-speakers, views her racial, linguistic, and intellectual identity through the white gaze in ways that negates her value.

Janel also describes the emotional harm and consequences enduring Anti-Black Linguistic Racism had on her sense of self and identity. She explains that when she was younger, she would "break down" when her teachers chastised her for communicating in Black Language because she felt they were trying to scrutinize her. Janel's experience captures how teachers are complicit in the reproduction of Anti-Black Linguistic Racism and "the debasement of black humanity, utter indifference to black suffering, and the denial of Black people's right to exist" (Jeffries, 2014). Similarly, Janel describes how upsetting it was to experience Anti-Black Linguistic Racism in the Black church—a social location that has historically nurtured and cultivated Black linguistic and cultural practices and a place that Janel associated with the biblical verse "do not judge or you too will be judged" (Matthew 7:1). Instead, Janel felt she was judged harshly by women she considered her elders simply because of how she talked. In addition to the emotional harm and indelible mark this experience left on her, Janel's experience offers an intersectional understanding of how her experience with Anti-Black Linguistic Racism is also impacted by her gender and class identity.

For example, the church women says that Janell is "gonna be a *rat*" and will turn out to be a "*baby mama.*" In the Black community, the lexical item *rat* is short for *hood rat* and describes a sexually promiscuous girl who lives in the hood (Smitherman, 1994). The lexical term *baby mama* emerged as a label to describe a child's mother, generally one who is not married to the child's father and is considered insignificant (Smitherman, 1994). Both rat and baby mama represent "a marked woman imbued with certain negative meanings in Black communities that often leaves her alienated" (Cooper, 2007, p. 322). The church women's chastisement of Janel's language can be seen as not only an attack on her language, but also a way to mark her Black, young female body outside of the norms of Black middle class culture (Cooper, 2007). Although white supremacy, anti-blackness, and misogynoir are the cause of this state of affairs, it is important to highlight Janel's experience with the church women as an example of how Anti-Black Linguistic Racism gets internalized and perpetuated within Black communities.

Although Janel and the women at her church were united by skin color and gender identification, their class was a different story. Janel captures the class difference between her and the church women by describing them as *boojee*, a lexical item within the Black speech community that often describes an "elitist, uppity-acting African American, generally with a higher educational and income level than the average Black, who identifies with European American culture and distances him/herself from other African Americans" (Smitherman, 1994, p. 76). To further illustrate their boujeeness, Janel uses the rhetorical strategy *signifyin* when she states, "*they was like all from 21 mile.*" Williams-Farrier (2016) defines signifyin as:

> a ritualized kind of put-down, an insult, a way of talking about, needling, or *signifyin on* someone else. Sometimes it's done just for fun, in conversations with friends and close associates. Other times, the put-down is used for a more serious purpose. In this communicative practice, the speaker deploys exaggeration, irony, and indirection as a way of saying something on two different levels at once.
>
> *(Williams-Farrier, 2016, p. 225)*

21 Mile is a road located in a suburb 13 miles north of Detroit. On one level, Janel is using the signifyin feature to communicate that the church women do not reside in Detroit. On another level, she uses this feature to suggest that the women are boujee, and prejudging her because she lives in Detroit and communicates in a language that reflects that community, which is majority Black and working class. It was not clear to me if Janel actually knew where the women resided, but what I find interesting is how far outside of the inner-city she places them. Janel could have simply stated that the women lived in the suburbs, but she intentionally uses 21 mile to signify or exaggerate how removed the women were from the inner-city. This comment not only suggests that the women were far removed from Detroit, but to also signify how far removed they were from the Black community, Black culture, Black Language, and blackness in general.

A Composite Character Counterstory about Allistar's Internalized Anti-Black Linguistic Racism

"Ok, bye Momma!" Allistar said as he jumped out of his family's blue minivan.

He looked down at his cell phone to check the time and immediately dashed through the metal double doors of LA once he realized he only had three minutes to make it to class. Allistar was an honors student and member of the varsity basketball team. He hated being late to his first hour because he knew Ms. Helen would tell his coach. On his way running to his locker, Allistar almost knocked a folder out of Janel's hand. As he approached his locker, he yelled to his lockermate, Fetti Bravo, "Aye man … leave dat open!"

"Yo! Did you see the game last night?" Fetti asked Allistar.
"Did I see it? What kinda question is that?" Allistar said as he put his coat in the locker. Allistar and Fetti were referencing the 2013 NBA Finals. "Man, Lebron gon' win that MVP award this year! Watch!" Allistar said.
"Nah, man, what is you talking about!?" Fetti responded. The boys went back and forth until they heard the bell ring. "Aww snap … we late!" Allistar said.

The boys grabbed their folders and ran to class. As they entered Ms. Helen's room, they were greeted by Ms. Baker-Bell. "Good morning! Y'all made it just in time for the first activity," she said as she handed them the stapled sheets of paper. As Allistar and Fetti sat down, Ms. Helen cleared her throat, making an "ahem" sound to get the boys' attention.

Allistar quickly responded, "My bad, Ms. Helen! My momma be running late in the morning."

"We'll talk about it after school. Come see me before practice." Ms. Helen replied and then turned to Ms. Baker-Bell and said "Although he said that in a non-eloquent way, he is really smart."

After seventh hour, Allistar and Fetti returned to Ms. Helen's class to discuss why they were late to class earlier.

"Ms. Helen had to meet with Ms. Lockett. She'll be back shortly," Ms. Baker-Bell said as she flipped through the stack of papers in front of her.

"Aight. Is it cool for us to wait in here?" Allistar asked.

"Sure," Ms. Baker-Bell replied. "Hey … while y'all waiting, can we talk about the activity we did in class today?"

"Oh, the good language, bad language stuff? Yeah, we can do that," Allistar responded. Fetti nodded in agreement.

"I noticed that you wrote that language shows one's knowledge, and a person who communicates in language A [Black Language] has little education," Ms. Baker-Bell said to Allistar. "Tell me more about your thinking about this."

"Well, when you speak like that. It shows you don't have knowledge because it's like you're not talking in complete sentences or you're not doing what they taught you at school," Allistar replied. "Usually when you see somebody who talk like that, they're a thug."

"Whatchu mean by thug?" Fetti asked.

"Someone who does not do the right thang. Someone who is constantly in trouble or in and out of jail. Someone who skip school. Don't get good grades," Allistar quickly answered.

"Have you ever been judged or labeled a thug when you're speaking like this?" Ms. Baker-Bell says as she looks at Allistar.

"If somebody was to walk by and hear me, possibly," Allistar responds with uncertainty.

"But what about you? You talk like that too! You consider yourself a thug?" Fetti quickly asked.

"Nah!" Allistar replied. "I'm not a hood person, but I live in the hood. I speak the hood or whatever. It's just usually when you see somebody talkin' like that, this is how they dress and look," Allistar said as he pointed at the image he drew to represent Black Language. "It's portrayed this way on tv and in movies too."

"My dad use both [Black Language and White Mainstream English], and he's educated and far from a thug. Just because you speak like that don't mean you got to be hood or ghetto," Fetti stated. "You can see people sagging their pants and hat backwards and they can use language A and B. It all depends."

"True. I guess I'm talking about people who use it all the time—there's a time and place." Allistar replied. "You don't want to go up in no interview saying 'what up?'" Allistar added.

"Is it ever an okay time to use language A?" Ms. Baker-Bell asked.

"Like my older brother. He in college right now. When he around his friends, he talk like that [Black Language]. But if he around certain people, he don't," Allistar responded.

"Yeah, that's the way I talk when I'm around my friends too. You don't have to say as many words. It's a shorter way to put stuff in a sentence," Fetti responded.

"So what influenced your thinking about when you should use this language?" Ms. Baker-Bell asked Allistar and Fetti as she pointed at the Black Language sample on the sheet in front of her.

"My momma and daddy. They told me not to speak like that," Allistar responded.

"My mom and school," Fetti followed up.

"My parents tell me not to speak like this because they don't want me and my siblings to go through what our daddy went through. He is from Trinidad and had a problem when he first came here [United States]. My mom had to teach him English so he could speak better and know what to say when looking for a job. Certain times, depending on where we go, some people might judge him and be like 'why he speaks like Caribbean?' or they sometimes say 'he's not from here.' They'll say little comments like that," Allistar added. "So if my parents hear me talking like that, they'll make me resay the sentence until I get it completely correct."

"Same! If I say something the wrong way, my mom will tell me to say something else. This happens at school too," Fetti said.

"Yep. In elementary school, I used to get away with talking like this, but once I got in middle school, I knew this was not the right way to talk."

"How did you know?" Ms. Baker-Bell asked.

"I attended an all-white school a couple years back, and no one talked in slang or sagged or anything like that," Allistar replied.

"What about now?" Ms. Baker-Bell queried.

"At this school, you usually don't hear kids talk like language B [White Mainstream English]. You usually hear them using language A [Black Language]."

"And what happens when you use language A here?" Ms. Baker-Bell asked.

"I get corrected. Especially in Math and English," Allistar responded. "Teachers treat you like you dumb when you talk like that. Like earlier when Ms. Helen said I speak in a non-eloquent way."

"How does that make you feel?" Ms. Baker-Bell asked.

"I always feel a little upset like, what is it? What am I doing wrong? And, how can I fix it?" Allistar answered.

As Allistar finished talking, Ms. Helen walked into the room and told the boys to meet her in the hall. When Allistar stands up, he says, "Maybe I should say … you should not be judged because you speak a certain way or dress a certain way. You should be judged by your character. Language A represents the type of people you around and the neighborhood you in. You speak your environment, I guess."

Reflecting on Allistar's Internalized Anti-Black Linguistic Racism

The composite character counterstory about Allistar's internalized Anti-Black Linguistic Racism is reflective of the initial attitudes and perspectives I observed among many of the students at LA as well as other Black youth I have interacted with during my teaching and research. Allistar's counterstory illustrates how he unconsciously supported white linguistic hegemony and perpetuated anti-blackness and Anti-Black Linguistic Racism. For instance, he continues to describe Black Language-speakers as intellectually and morally inferior: "little education," "don't have knowledge," "don't get good grades," "in and out of jail," "not speaking in complete sentences," "skip school," "trouble," etc. Yet, he characterizes speakers of White Mainstream English as "very smart" and "striving for the best." Charity Hudley and Mallinson (2014) remind us that youth who absorb messages that suggest that their language is wrong, incorrect, dumb, or stigmatized may react with internalization, which is "a process whereby members of stigmatized groups accept negative messages about their self-worth" (p. 65). Unlike the resistance we observed in Janel's counterstory, we do not see instances of Allistar pushing back against Anti-Black Linguistic Racism or white linguistic hegemony. In fact, Allistar does not begin to reconsider his thinking until Fetti challenges his assumptions and stereotypes about speakers of Black Language, which illustrates the importance of creating space for Black students to engage in dialogic consciousness-raising.

The composite character counterstory of Allistar also reveals that many of the Black students were aware that the "value attributed to particular languages is intimately tied to larger understandings of race and racial hierarchy in U.S. society" (Bedolla, 2003, p. 265). For example, the image Allistar drew to represent speakers of Black Language included a sideways baseball cap, sagging pants, and an Afro, which are cultural markers distinct to the Black community (see Figure 3.2). Like many of Allistar's peers' drawings, the image associated with White Mainstream English included a "suit and tie" and "eyeglasses." Reminiscent of Kirkland and Jackson's (2008) study, there was "an aura of success that pervaded the White Mainstream English character and an air of accomplishment was artistically woven onto the image" (p. 141). I also want to point out that Allistar and many of his peers associated fashions that are rooted in Black culture with inferiority, which illustrates how Black students oftentimes view "themselves as *other* through the dominant gaze" (Hayes, 2015, p. 16).

As argued by Pritchard (2017), fashion and literacy are interlocking systems of expression that provide youth a space to self-create, self-affirm, and adorn oneself with a sense of belonging. Fashion offers "an analysis of intervention into systems of power and domination historically, sociologically, economically, and rhetorically" (p. 127). With this in mind, Pritchard encourages teachers and researchers to think more seriously about "the role of dress in literacy history, theory, and praxis as fashion is a useable surface on which to explore the seamlessness between the word and the world" (p. 129). Pritchard's exploration of fashion literacies helps to shed light on the value that's placed on fashion within many Black communities, especially among Black youth within those communities. From hoodies to head scarves, *what* Black people wear and how *we* wear it matters! Although cultural markers such as "sagging," "backward and sideways baseball caps," "head scarves," "beaters," and "white tees" are perceived negatively by dominant culture and older generations, this is not necessarily the attitude held among Black youth. For them, natural hairstyles and sagging communicate their fashion sense and symbolize freedom, cultural awareness, or their rejection to the values held by mainstream society (Hayes, 2015).

Allistar's criticism of Black Language, culture, and fashions were heartbreaking, yet unsurprising given the ways that anti-blackness and white linguistic and cultural hegemony get upheld in our schools, homes, communities, curriculum, classrooms, and society in general. But perhaps what was most troubling about Allistar's criticism of Black Language was that it disclosed traces of his unconscious negative view of himself and other Black people. For example, the clothing of the character he constructed to represent Black Language ironically resembled the fashions I observed him and many of his peers wearing on Free Dress Friday.[2] That is, many of the boys wore sagging pants, white tees, jewelry chains, and designer shoes. Further, as illustrated in his written response to the activity, he used grammatical features of Black Language to admonish the character he constructed to represent Black Language all while singing the praises of the character he constructed to represent White Mainstream English. When I first read Allistar's remarks, I was left with many questions: Did Allistar realize he was utilizing many of the same linguistic features as the character he drew to reflect Black Language? Why did Allistar think the character he constructed to represent Black Language look like a thug if he sported similar fashions? Allistar was an honors student who used Black Language, so why did he think Black Language-speakers have "little education" based solely on their language? The answers to these questions magnify Richardson's (2004) argument that when Black students are taught to hate Black speech, it indirectly teaches them to hate themselves.

Allistar's composite character counterstory also illustrates that school is not the only place where white linguistic hegemony and Anti-Black Linguistic Racism is perpetuated. Allistar, Fetti, Janel, and many of their peers stated that their parents would correct them when they used Black Language, which indicates that Black Language is not completely valued in the context of home. As emphasized by

Kirkland and Jackson (2008), Black Language is not seen as socially or intellectually valuable even in the context of family. Indeed, many Black parents have also endured what Smitherman refers to as the "cycle of miseducation." That is, children are not taught in their language arts classrooms that all human languages and language varieties have inherent grammatical patterns and are systematic and rule-governed. Instead, linguistic miseducation will occur through their teachers' obsession with teaching "correct" grammar, spelling, and pronunciation. These children will grow up to be mis-educated adults. (Smitherman, 2017, p. 6). Adults mis-educated about language will pass this miseducation, color-evasiveness, and white linguistic hegemony onto others, including their children. In addition to miseducation, some parents, like Allistar's, believe that they are protecting their children from the linguistic violence they endured as children by teaching them to adhere to respectability politics and not use Black Language. They do not realize that this is actually interfering with their children's language and literacy learning. This further illustrates how Black Language-speakers internalize Anti-Black Linguistic Racism under the cloak of whiteness and underscores the need for researchers and teachers to consider the role of parents and family as we re-educate Black students about their language.

Janel's and Allistar's composite character counterstories provide an in-depth look into how Black students are impacted by Anti-Black Linguistic Racism. Their counterstories affirm that eradicationist and respectability language pedagogies do not account for the internalized Anti-Black Linguistic Racism, linguistic double consciousness, or the consequences these approaches have on Black students' sense of self and identities. Their voices and perspectives beg for an alternative language education that provides them with an alternative way of looking at Black Language. In the following chapter, I will lay out the Antiracist Black Language Pedagogy that I engaged the students at LA in, which is an essential step in getting Black students to unlearn anti-blackness and Anti-Black Linguistic Racism.

Notes

1 The samples included under language A were patterns that I heard students using at LA during the observation phase of the study.
2 A Friday where students were able to wear clothes outside of the school uniform.

References

Albers, P., Holbrook, T., & Flint, A. (Eds.) (2013). *New Methods in Literacy Research*. New York, NY: Routledge.

Alim, H. S., & Smitherman, G. (2012). *Articulate While Black: Barack Obama, Language, and Race in the U.S.* Oxford, NY: Oxford University Press.

Baker-Bell, A., Paris, D., & Jackson, D. (2017) Learning Black Language Matters: Humanizing research as culturally sustaining pedagogy. *International Review of Qualitative Research*, 10(4), 360–377.

Bedolla, G. J. (2003). The identity paradox: Latino language, politics and selective dissociation. *Latino Studies*, 1(2), 264–283.

Charity Hudley, M., & Mallinson, C. (2014). *We do Language. English Language Variation in the Secondary English Classroom*. New York, NY: Teachers College Press.

Cook, D. (2013). Blurring the boundaries. The mechanics of creating composite characters. In M. Lynn & A. Dixon (Eds.), *Handbook of Critical Race Theory in Education* (pp. 181–194). New York: Routledge.

Cooper, B. (2007). Excavating the love below: The state as patron of the baby mama drama and other ghetto hustles. In G. Pough, E. Richardson, A. Durham, & R. Raimist (Eds.), *Home Girls Make Some Noise: Hip Hop Feminism Anthology* (pp. 320–344). Mira Loma, CA: Parker Publishing, LLC.

Hayes, S. (2015). "S.W.A.G. = Style with a goal": Exploring fashion/style as a critical literacy of Black youth in urban schools (Doctoral Dissertation). Retrieved from ProQuest.

hooks, b. (1992). *Black Looks: Race and Representation*. Boston, MA: South End Press.

Jeffries, M. (2014, November 28). Ferguson must force us to face anti-blackness. *Boston Globe*. Retrieved from https://www.bostonglobe.com/opinion/2014/11/28/ferguson-must-force-face-anti-Blackness/pKVMpGxwUYpMDyHRWPln2M/story.html

Kirkland, D. E., & Jackson, A. (2008). Beyond the silence: Instructional approaches and students' attitudes. In J. Scott, D. Y. Straker, & L. Katz (Eds.), *Affirming Students' Right to Their Own Language: Bridging Educational Policies and Language/Language Arts Teaching Practices* (pp. 160–180). Urbana, IL: NCTE/LEA.

Paris, D., & Alim, H. S. (Eds.). (2017). *Culturally Sustaining Pedagogies: Teaching and Learning for Justice in a Changing World*. New York, NY: Teachers College Press.

Paris, D., & Ball, A. (2011). African American Language in U.S. education and society: A story of success and failure. In J. Fishman & O. Garcia (Eds.), *Handbook of Language & Ethnic Identity: The Success-Failure Continuum in Language and Ethnic Identity Efforts* (Volume2) (pp. 85–95). Oxford: Oxford University Press.

Pritchard, D. E. (2017). *Fashioning Lives: Black Queers and the Politics of Literacy*. Carbondale, IL: Southern Illinois University Press.

Richardson, E. (2004). Coming from the heart: African American students, literacy stories, and rhetorical education. In E. Richardson & R. Jackson (Eds.), *African American Rhetoric(s): Interdisciplinary Perspectives* (pp. 155–169). Carbondale, IL: Southern Illinois University Press.

Rickford J. R., & Rickford, R. J. (2000). *Spoken Soul: The Story of Black English*. New York, NY: Wiley.

Smitherman, G. (1977). *Talkin and Testifyin: The Language of Black America*. Detroit, MI: Wayne State University Press.

Smitherman, G. (1994). *Black talk: Words and Phrases from the Hood to the Amen Corner*. New York, NY: Houghton Mifflin.

Smitherman, G. (1998). Ebonics, King, and Oakland: Some folk don't believe fat meat is greasy. *Journal of English Linguistics*, 26(2), 97–107.

Smitherman, G. (2017). Raciolinguistics, "mis-education," and language arts teaching in the 21st century. *Language Arts Journal of Michigan*, 32(2), 4–12.

Solorzano, D., & Yosso, T. (2002). Critical race methodology: Counter-storytelling as an analytical framework for education. *Qualitative Inquiry*, 8(1), 23–44.

Williams-Farrier, B. (2016). Signifying, narrativizing, and repetition: Radical approaches to theorizing African American language. *Meridians*, 15, 218–242.

4

"SCOFF NO MORE"

I titled this chapter "Scoff No More" because it is a direct response to the point Carter G. Woodson made in 1933 about Black students being taught to despise their mother tongue instead of learning about it and Geneva Smitherman's call for critical language awareness.

> In the study of language in school pupils were made to scoff at the Negro dialect as some peculiar possession of the Negro which they should despise rather than directed to study the background of this language as a broken-down African tongue—in short to understand their own linguistic history, which is certainly more important for them than the study of French Phonetics or Historical Spanish Grammar.
>
> *(Woodson, 1933, p. 10)*

> Critical Language Awareness pedagogy seeks to develop in students a critical consciousness about language, power, and society. It seeks to heighten their awareness of the stakes involved in language attitude and policies of correctness and strives to impart knowledge about their own language, its social and linguistic rules, its history and cultural connection. Instead of just accepting language as a gate-keeping check on race and ethnicity, instead of capitulating to "that's just the way things are," … Critical Language Awareness pedagogy helps students examine and account for why things are the way they are.
>
> *(Smitherman, 2017, p. 10)*

In the spirit of linguistic justice, this chapter shows the praxis of the Antiracist Black Language Pedagogy, specifically illustrating how I used critical consciousness-raising to help the students at Leadership Academy (LA) challenge, interrogate, unlearn, and work toward dismantling Anti-Black Linguistic Racism. Chapter 4 has two major functions. As a resource for language and literacy educators, this chapter illuminates what an Antiracist Black Language Pedagogy looks like on the ground (aka in the classroom). For language and literacy researchers, it illuminates how theory, research, and practice can operate in tandem in pursuit of linguistic and racial justice. This chapter also offers ethnographic snapshots of how Black students responded to some of the Black Language Artifacts that comprised the Antiracist Black Language Pedagogy. As you read this chapter, I ask you to consider the following questions: Why is it pivotal for Black students to learn about their own linguistic backgrounds? In what ways are the students beginning to critically interrogate and consistently resist white linguistic hegemony and Anti-Black Linguistic Racism?

The sections that follow are divided by Black Language Artifacts 2–7. Under each artifact, I provide a background component that explains information that foregrounds each artifact. Next, I provide a description of the artifacts and include an ethnographic snapshot (when available) that reveals how the students at LA responded to the various topics. I also include materials (worksheets, resources, links, etc.) that I used to engage the students.

"I Never Knew the History Behind Black Language": The Historical Underpinnings of Black Language Matters

Background

Five hundred years ago, European enslavers and African middlemen raided villages and homes in various parts of Africa to abduct African people for the Transatlantic Slave Trade. In addition to kidnapping, beating, abusing, and sexually exploiting African people, enslavers used *language planning* as a tool to separate captive Africans who spoke the same language as a way to minimize rebellion (Baugh, 2015). Women, men, and children were separated from their loved ones and loaded onto slave ships leaving behind their freedom, their humanity, their homelands, their families, their cultural traditions, and their languages. After a traumatic journey from West Africa to the New World, enslaved Africans who survived the Middle Passage arrived to the Caribbean, the Americas, and various parts of Europe chained together, without a shared language to communicate with one another, or the ability to communicate in their oppressor's language (Baugh, 2015). In her book *Teaching to Transgress: Education as the Practice of Freedom*, hooks (1994) thinks about the trauma enslaved Africans must have felt about the loss of their language and the terrifying sound of the English language:

> I think now of the grief of displaced "homeless" Africans, forced to inhabit a world where they saw folks like themselves, inhabiting the same skin, the same condition, but who had no shared language to talk with one another,

who needed the oppressor's language … When I imagine the terror of Africans on board slave ships, on auction blocks, inhabiting the unfamiliar architecture of plantations, consider that this terror extended beyond fear of punishment, that it resided also in the anguish of hearing a language they could not comprehend.

(hooks, 1994, p. 169)

In addition to linguistic isolation, enslaved Africans who were dispersed in the United States were intentionally denied access to literacy by law. Still, they needed to learn the language of the land to help build the physical, cultural, and intellectual foundations of this nation (Thomas, 2018). Despite losing contact with their native language and it being illegal to teach them to read and write, enslaved Africans created a language out of remnants of their mother tongues and pieces and parts of the English language. This language not only provided a way for enslaved Africans to communicate among each other, but it also provided the means of communication that could not be fully understood by their oppressors (Baldwin, 1979). Fast forward to today, Black Americans are being penalized for using the counter-language that their ancestors were forced to create instead of White Mainstream English, the language of conquest and domination (hooks, 1994; Baugh, 2015).

As hooks points out, an "unbroken connection exists between the broken English of the displaced, enslaved African and the diverse Black vernacular speech Black folks use today" (hooks, 1994, p. 171). Yet, as Woodson noted in 1933, this connection and linguistic history is not typically included in the language education that Black students, or any student, receive in school. Smitherman (2006) argues that:

[The] lack of knowledge about our history … is at the root of the problem of miseducation of Black youth today. They have no sense of their role and purpose in history, no understanding of where they came from, and consequently, no vision for where they're going.

(Smitherman, 2006, p. 143)

Learning about the history of Black Language matters! Within broader discussions about enslavement, there is not much discussion about language. By ignoring this deep connection, we are not only contributing to the miseducation of Black students, but we are also contributing to an oppressive structure that serves as the catalyst to the erasure of Black linguistic history.

Black Language Artifact 2: Language, History, and Culture

Black Language Artifact 2 was created in response to Woodson's 87-year-old call to teach Black kids about the history of their native language. In this section, I illustrate how I translated the linguistic history underpinning Black Language into a learning experience that was accessible to the students at LA. I also provide ethnographic snapshots of how the students responded to the artifact. Before jumping into the activity, the students and I reflected on their responses to the attitudinal assessment that they completed under Black Language Artifact #1, and we discussed their background knowledge about Black Language.

> "How many of you know that language sample A is an actual language?" I asked.
> Many of the students nodded in response to my question.
> "Do you know the name of the language?" I asked.
> "Slang," a few of the students said in unison.
> "Well ... slang is not a language. Slang is almost like a style of speaking that is generational or goes in and out of style. Whereas a language is a rule-based linguistic system," I replied. "We will complete an activity in a few days that will help us explore this further. Does anyone else know what the name for language sample A is?" I asked.
> "Ebonics," Fetti blurted.
> "Ebonics! That's right," I responded.
> "Didn't Ebonics come from slaves?" Fetti asked.

What is striking about my discussion with the students is that it reveals that only one student actually knew the name for his native language—though it has roots as deep and grammar as consistent as Scottish English, Irish English, and other world Englishes (Baugh, 2015), and it was once the most studied and written about variety of English in the world (Gilyard, 2005).

Our discussion made for an organic segue way into the inquiry-based activity I developed to immerse the students in a language study that examined the historical underpinnings of Black Language. As seen in Figure 4.1, the worksheet was a conversation about the history of Black Language, and it included three characters that were designed to contribute a specific point of view to the discussion. For example, the first character in Figure 4.1 states, "But Black Language seems unprofessional, ghetto, and uneducated in comparison to White Mainstream English?" This character represents the uniformed perspective of Black Language typically held by the general public and was initially held by the students at LA. The second character in the conversation was created to interrogate dominant assumptions about language. That character questions, "Why is Black Language always treated as if it is the 'good-for-nothing' cousin of the English language—as if it has no rules, and is substandard to White Mainstream English? Isn't Black Language linked to the enslavement of African people? We hardly ever talk about the history of Black Language or its richness and how it reflects the ingenuity on the part of enslaved Africans." The third character in the conversation was positioned as the knowledge holder that provided an informed perspective about Black Language's linguistic history, which I included in the background section above. Finally, the worksheet includes a blank section that provides space for the students to contribute their ideas, thoughts, and perspectives to the conversation.

The students responded to this activity in a variety of ways. Most of them were bewildered after learning about the rich history of Black Language. The most common response to the activity was "I never knew that Black Language was a mixture of Black English and White Mainstream English." Other students such as Lola questioned "why people don't let us use Black Language?" Allistar commented "I did not know we spoke like that. I think the language should be preserved because this language helped us form American culture."

Following our discussion about the activity, I provided the students with additional historical context about Black Language. In particular, we discussed language planning, the origins of Black Language, and coded spirituals. I discuss each of these topics more in detail in the section below, and I include the supplemental resources I used to provide the students with an extensive understanding of the topic.

Language Planning

I began discussing language planning by explaining how the institution of slavery would not have been successful without language planning. Baldwin states "If two black people, at that bitter hour of the world's history, had been able to speak to each other, the institution of chattel slavery could never have lasted as long as it did" (p. 1). I used John Baugh's (2015) article *Use and misuse speech diagnostics for African American students* to provide the students with an in-depth understanding of the function of language planning during enslavement. Baugh explains that:

> slave traders routinely separated slaves by language whenever possible upon capture. This practice of isolating recent captives who shared a common language was intended to minimize uprisings; if [enslaved Africans] had a harder time communicating, they were less likely to be able to organize revolts. This form of "language planning" was intended to isolate the enslaved African captives from the language(s) they knew and used. Moreover, this linguistic isolation began in West Africa prior to the Atlantic crossing, and as a result of these efforts, no African language survived the Atlantic crossing completely intact.

I then prompted students to think about how enslaved Africans were thrust into a linguistic situation where they lost their relationship with their native language but had to learn the English language. The students were eager to know how enslaved Africans developed Black Language if they did not know the English language and were linguistically separated as a result of language planning. This led to a discussion about the origins of Black Language.

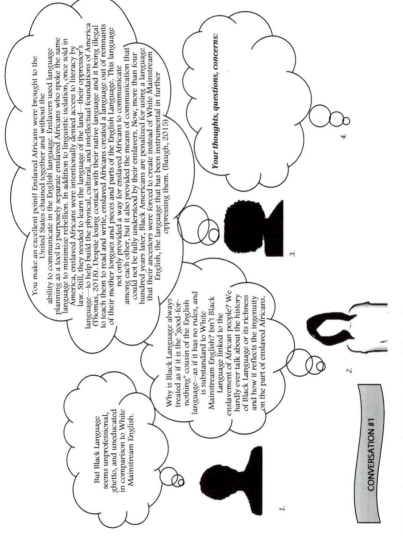

FIGURE 4.1 Conversation about Black Language Worksheet #1

Origins of Black Language

To begin our discussion about how enslaved Africans developed their own language, I used Lisa Green's (2002) book *African American English* to provide the students with historical accounts of the development and origins of Black Language. We began the conversation by discussing how some linguists believe that Black Language is a hybrid of English and West African Languages. According to Green (2002):

> Some historical accounts of the development of AAE [or African American English] have taken the position that the distinctive patterns of AAE are those which also occur in Niger-Congo languages such as Kikongo, Mande, and Kwa. In effect, the view is that AAE is structurally related to West African languages.
>
> *(Green, 2002, pp. 8–9)*

Smitherman (2006) confirms this when she states, "a dominant African linguistic presence survived in the African style of speaking; in other words, using English words with an African linguistic FLAVA" (p. 19). I build on this discussion by having students watch a short clip from the 2005 documentary *We Speak American*. [1] In the clip, linguist John Baugh explains the practice of language planning and the early origins of what we now call Black Language.

After we watched the clip, many of the students were curious about how enslaved Africans cultivated Black Language, especially in the face of enslavement. To explore their curiosities, I had the students come up with their own theories about how the language evolved. We then read a few pages from the introduction to Smitherman's (1994) Black dictionary, *Black Talk*. I used the reading to emphasize Smitherman's salient point about the Black church and Black music being two significant forces that have nurtured and preserved African cultural traditions. Baldwin (1979) explains that enslaved Africans "began the formation of the Black church, and it is within this unprecedented tabernacle that Black English began to be formed" (p. 1) Indeed, the Black church functioned as a social and religious unit that "has stood as a rich reservoir of terms and expressions in Black Language ... [because] it has not had to capitulate to the sociocultural pressure of Eurocentric culture and the language of white folk" (Smitherman, 1994, pp. 22–23). We also discussed Smitherman's insight about Black music being a major force in the formation and development of words and phrases within the Black speech community. We had an opportunity to explore this insight more when we discussed coded negro spirituals.

A Counter-language

After discussing the origins and development, I had the students read bell hooks' chapter titled "Language: Teaching New Worlds/ New Words" from her book

Teaching to Transgress to give them perspective about how traumatic and dehumanizing the practice of language planning and its aftermath was for enslaved Africans. The chapter also helped the students understand how enslaved Africans reinvented and remade the English language to speak beyond the boundaries of conquest and domination. hooks (1994) explains:

> In the mouths of Black Africans in the so-called "New World," English was altered, transformed and became a different speech. Enslaved Black people took broken bits of English and made of them a counter-language. They put together their words in such a way that the colonizer had to rethink the meaning of the English Language. Though it has become common in contemporary culture to talk about the messages of resistance that emerged in the music created by [enslaved Africans], particularly spirituals, less is said about the grammatical structure of sentences in these songs. Often, the English used in the song reflected the broken, ruptured word of the slave.
>
> *(hooks, 1994, p. 170)*

This passage allowed for me to show the students how Black Language functions as a counter-language that allows the communication of simultaneous double meanings. To back this up, I had the students read and interpret the coded negro spirituals *Wade in the Water, Swing Low Sweet Chariot,* and *Steal Away to Jesus* to make sense of how the covert messages were being passed through spirituals to facilitate escape.

Following this activity, we watched a short clip on coded spirituals.[2] The clip, narrated by author and public historian Rev. Velma Maia Thomas, breaks down some of the coded messages represented in the spirituals. For example, she explains how the coded spiritual *Wade in the Water* contained hidden meanings that signaled to escaping enslaved Africans to get off the trail and into the water so that the dogs used by enslavers could not pick up on their scent. hooks (1994) posits:

> even as emancipated Black people sang spirituals, they did not change the language … of our ancestors. For the incorrect usage of words, in the incorrect placement of words, was a spirit of rebellion that claimed language as a site of resistance.
>
> *(hooks, 1994, p. 70)*

I also included the following passage from James Baldwin's (1979) *New York Times* article to help us think more about language as a site of rebellion:

> There was a moment, in time, and in this place, when my brother, or my mother, or my father, or my sister, had to convey to me, for example, the danger in which I was standing from the white man standing just behind me, and to convey this with a speed, and in a language, that the white man could

not possibly understand, and that, indeed, he cannot understand, until today. He cannot afford to understand it. This understanding would reveal to him too much about himself, and smash that mirror before which he has been frozen for so long.

This passage from Baldwin helped us think more deeply about why it was necessary for Black Language to be a linguistic survival strategy and how it was a tool for enslaved Africans and their descendants to resist, rebel, and reclaim their power in the context of domination.

"Ebonically Speaking": An Antiracist Approach to Teaching the Grammatical and Rhetorical Underpinnings of Black Language

Background

Black Language is a complicated linguistic system that "crosses boundaries of age, gender, region, religion, and social class" (Smitherman, 1994, p. 1), and it is spoken by millions of Black people in the U.S. Though Black Language is viewed as a symbol of linguistic and intellectual inferiority and is devalued, despised, and rejected in many classrooms, communities, and sometimes in the context of home, like "every naturally used language, Black Language is systematic with regular rules and restrictions at the lexical, phonological and grammatical level" (Rickford, 2002, p. 1). As discussed previously, Black Language is not merely "a set of deviations from the 'standard'" that can be classified as solely slang or street talk. Just like the slang in every language, Black slang is transitory and represents the new and short-lived vocabulary of Black Language. For example, the word *drip*, as in *his outfit is full of drip*, is a slang item in Black Language used among younger generations. Smitherman (1994) posits that "Black slang is Black Language, but all Black Language is not Black slang" (p. 2). In fact, Black Language encompasses words (*ashy*), distinctive patterns of pronunciation (*mah/my*), and grammar that are more systematic (*They be at home),* deeply rooted, and stable over time. In addition to its grammar, meaning, and sound, Black Language is unique for its rich rhetorical style. Features such as signifyin', semantic inversion, and call & response are a few examples of the Black cultural modes of discourse that have survived for generations in the Black community.

Though linguists have produced detailed accounts of the pronunciation and grammatical system of Black Language since at least the 1960s (Rickford & Rickford, 2000), Black children are often not formally taught the linguistic features of their own language in the context of school. It is well known within multilingual education that literacy development and language learning should not happen at the expense of the loss of one's mother tongue. Black students are not exempt from this theory although they are often excluded from it. Undoubtedly, there are numerous examples of Black students' linguistic features being viewed from a deficit perspective with the goal to eradicate it and replace it with White Mainstream English. However, Smitherman (2017) argues:

> Students will end up being mis-educated about language if they aren't taught that all human languages and language varieties (yes, even African American Language and Arabic!) have inherent grammatical patterns and are systematic and rule-governed. Even though humans are "born to speak," that is, language is a part of human beings' genetic make-up, they are not born speaking a particular Language.
>
> *(Smitherman, 2017, p. 6)*

In the section below, I describe how I used a critical and cultural approach to teach the students at LA the rules of our native tongue.

Black Language Artifact 3: Study of the Grammatical and Rhetorical Features of Black Language

Black Language Artifact 3 was created in the spirit of putting the linguistic knowledge back in the hands of the linguistic community that owns it. In other words, what good is linguistic research on Black Language if it is not reaching the community it is intended to serve? In the face of Anti-Black Linguistic Racism, it is not only necessary for Black students to know that they are communicating in a valid linguistic system, but it is just as important for them to be able to pinpoint and name the features of their own linguistic system. As seen in Figure 4.2, the language instruction began with the students engaging in an inquiry-based activity I developed to immerse them in a conversation about the grammatical structure and rhetorical features of the language.

The students' responses to this activity revealed so much about their previous language education. Lola wrote the following comment on her sheet: "I did not know it was good definitions to Black Language. I always thought it was bad." Chasse wrote: "I never knew that it was legitimate. I also didn't know that it was connected with a history of oppression." Other comments included: "I thought the way African Americans talked could be considered street talk or slang, but I also noticed that different races used this type of language also." The students' comments illustrate that Black Language is not acknowledged as a valid, rule-based linguistic system in their curriculum nor is it treated as a linguistic resource that is necessary for their language and literacy development, to maintain relationships with family and community, to feel assured in their sense of self, or to express their identity.

When discussing the features of Black Language, I was careful not to reinforce culturally irresponsible approaches to language instruction by treating the students at LA as if they were not experts of their native language. They use the language everyday just like me; therefore, I wanted our study of the grammatical and

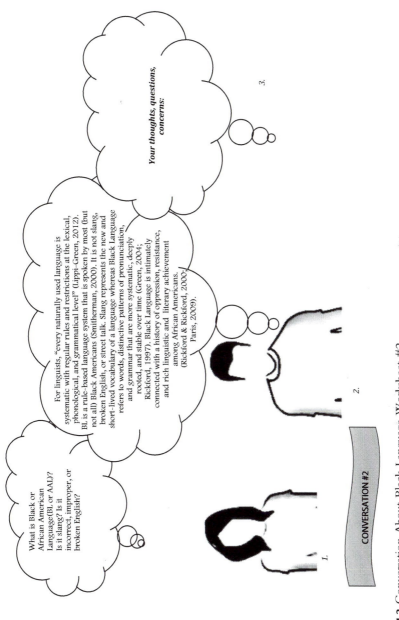

FIGURE 4.2 Conversation About Black Language Worksheet #2

rhetorical features to reflect our collective knowledge. To begin our language study, I displayed the features shown in Figure 4.3 on the projector screen which included patterns of Black Language and terminology that is typically used by linguists to describe those patterns. For each feature, we discussed its function, meaning, and a speaker's intention for using it. I include a snapshot of our discussion in the section below.

"I want to remind you all that we are not discussing these features because they are wrong. Just like there are rules and structure to languages like Spanish and French, there are rules to Black Language. There is a right and wrong way to use Black Language too," I said as the students' eyes were fixated on the projector screen.

"These are not all of the rules, but just some of the features to get us talking about the structure of the language. So let's look at the first sentence," I said as I pointed at the screen.

"*Habitual Be* is a pattern in Black Language. We *be* at Rouge Park hoopin' on Saturdays. What does the verb 'be' mean in this sentence?" I asked the students.

"It means that's what you do," I heard a voice from the back of the room say.

"But on the real Ms. Baker-Bell, don't nobody be hoopin at Rouge Park[3] no more," Fetti said.

(We all laughed.)

"I know. I know," I laughed. "They did back in my day, though."

"But, why is the *'be'* there," I asked the students again.

"It's like … it happens on a regular basis. They play at Rouge all the time on Saturdays," Allistar responded.

"So what happens if we change the verb *'be'* in the sentence to *'are'* as in 'We are at Rouge hoopin,'" I questioned.

"Then it means you are there hoopin right now.," Janel suggested.

"Okay what changed about the sentence," I said.

"It's no longer something you do all the time," Lola answered.

"Right, so this feature is important because …" Before I could finish, Chasse cut me off and said, "It is needed to explain when you are always doing something."

"Exactly! So let's look at the sentence under zero copula. It says, '*You right about that.*' Let's look at it and see what's goin on with it," I said.

"In White Mainstream English, you'd be expected to say 'You *ARE* right about that,'" Janel responded. (Emphasis hers)

"Right, but in Black Language it's perfectly fine to not use the '*are*,'" I said. "It communicates the same message, right? Remember what Baldwin said about Black Language? One of its functions is to communicate a message with speed."

SYNTAX	SEMANTICS	PRONUNCIATION	RHETORICAL FEATURES
Habitual Be We be at Rouge Park hoopin' on Saturdays. **Regularized Agreement** We was at Lisa's house last night. He have to be at work in the morning. **Zero Copula** You right about that. **Multiple Negation** I ain't got no friends at that school. **Den** It's too late. He done already paid for the trip. **BIN** We been done with our project. **Optional Possessive 'S** I'm going to my father house for the summer.	**Words & Idioms** Ashy Saddity Triflin Fake it til' you make it Tryin' to make a dollaout of fifteen cent. **Slang** Swag Keep it 100 Mood Fleek Issa Vibe Drip Goals	**Consonants** Aks or Axe (ask) **Final Consonant Clusters** Han (hand) Tes (test) **Sounds** Dey (They) Dese(These) Dem(Them) Wit or Wif (With) Smoov (Smooth) Baf (Bath)	**Signifyin** Do it look like money grow on trees? **Derrick**: "I be kickin' it with all the girls in seventh hour." **Sean**: "Yeah right! The only thing that be kickin' in seventh hour is yo breath." **Signifyin** Her outfit is badd! Nah, that's my nigga right there.

FIGURE 4.3 Features of Black Language

"That's rightttt. It's a quicker way of communicating," Lola responded.

"So as you all can see. There are several rules to Black Language. Instead of calling it 'slang,' 'ghetto,' or 'street talk,' we are going to acknowledge it as a language in its own right by referring to it as Black Language, African American Language, Ebonics, etc."

Our conversation about the remaining features of the language mirrors this snapshot. As illustrated in the above snapshot, my approach to grammar was not prescriptive nor did it involve me simply telling the students how language works. Instead, my approach involved the students observing, exploring, describing, and discussing language based on the literacies they have of their native language. For the purposes of this chapter functioning as both a window into how the students at LA engaged the Antiracist Black Language Pedagogy and a resource that put teachers up on game, I offer an overview of each feature listed in Figure 4.3.

Rickford & Rickford (2000) note that while there is still much to be uncovered about the linguistic features and attributes of Black Language, linguists already know enough to present an informed picture. I present some of what is known about the syntax, semantics, and phonology of Black Language below.

Syntax

Syntax refers to the arrangement of words and phrases to create well-formed sentences in a language.

- **Habitual Be** *(also known as invariant be)*: The habitual be is one of the most celebrated features of Black Language. It indicates habitual meaning or a recurring state or activity and suggests that something regularly or usually happens. The be incorporates past, present, and future activity. Examples used by the students at LA: *Everybody be talking like that.*
- **Regularized Agreement** (also known as absence of third person singular present-tense S): Within the Black speech community, third-person singular verbs do not require third-person singular subjects as in *"It seem."* Regularized agreement is also being used in this example by Allistar: *He don't want anything.*
- **Zero Copula** (also known as copula absence): Oftentimes marked by linguists using this symbol Ø, the copula verbs are not required in some instances within the Black speech community. Here is an example used by a student at LA: I picked her because she Ø nice and calm.
- **Multiple Negation**: Green (2002) explains that multiple negators such as *don't, no,* and *nothing* can be used in a single sentence. The pattern can be illustrated in the following example: *I ain't got no friends at this school.*
- **Dən**: The dən feature, pronounced *done*, marks the completed nature of an action, and/or its relevance to the present. An example of the dən feature is shown here: *He done already paid for the trip.*

- **BIN**: The stressed BIN feature, pronounced as been, is used to mark the remote past, as in *we been done without our project*. The way been is used in this sentence does not make it clear how long it's been since the project was complete. It could have been completed 2 hours ago or 2 days ago. How long it's actually been since the project was completed is not the speaker's purpose; rather, the purpose is to communicate that the activity occurred in the remote past.
- **Optional Possessive 'S** (also known as absence of possessive 'S): Black Language users do not have to rely on 's to indicate possession; instead, the juxtaposition of two nouns indicate possession (as in father house).

Semantics

Semantics is concerned with the meaning of words and word relations. There are certain words and phrases that carry unique meaning in the Black speech community. When I discussed semantics with the students at LA, I brought in a copy of Smitherman's (1994) Black dictionary *Black Talk: Words and Phrases from the Hood to the Amen Corners,* and let the students read through it. Many of them were astonished to learn, in Allistar's words, "that there is an actual dictionary for the way that my people talk."

- **Ashy**: describes the whitish, grayish, or dryish appearance of skin due to exposure to wind, cold, or not using moisturizer.
- **Fake it til' you make it**: Have confidence in whatever it is that you are doing until it becomes your reality.
- **Saditty**: describes a snooty, uppity-acting person.
- **Trying to make a dolla out of fifteen cent**: Trying to make ends meet with little financial resources.
- **Triflin/Trife**: Describes a person who fails to do something that they are capable of doing; irresponsible; out of pocket.

Slang

For the slang section, I had a discussion with the students about the kind of slang they were using at the time. They offered the following words and descriptions:

- **Swag**: a person who dresses cool and acts cool.
- **Keep it 100**: Keep it real; be honest.
- **Vibe**: Feeling, atmosphere, energy, positivity.

Phonology

Phonology describes the system of sounds within the Black Language system. Rickford & Rickford (2000) explains that the pronunciation of consonants often distinguishes Black Language from the ways that other ethnic groups in the United States speak.

- *Ask* (pronounced as aks or axe) is one of those distinguishing features. This feature is widely stigmatized and is often seen as a reflection of poor speech.
- There are also some consonants in White Mainstream English that are not present in Black Language and there are some consonants that are replaced. For example *han/hand* and *des/desk*. Additionally, there are some consonants that are replaced like in the case of *th* by *t, f, d,* **or** *v,* as in *they/dey, bath/baf, with/wif, smooth/smoov.*
- There are also voiceless final consonant clusters like *pt* (as in *kep/kept), st* (as in *bes/best), ld* (as in *col/cold), ct* (as in *ac/act), ft* (as in *lef/left),* and *nd* (as in *spen/spend).*

Rhetorical Features

Oftentimes language scholars and language teachers get so caught up on the grammatical properties of Black Language that they overlook the rich rhetorical features, also referred to as cultural modes of discourse. I describe a few of these features below.

- *Signifyin*: This feature describes a genre of linguistic performance in the Black speech community that allows for the communication of multiple levels of simultaneous meaning, usually involving wordplay and misdirection. Black Americans have used signifyin as a vehicle to express Black cultural knowledge, humor, or a serious social critique. For Black Americans navigating hostile and racial oppression, signifyin has offered a site of resistance and allowed double-voiced and encoded communication. Just as important as what is said is how it is said. Signifyin requires verbal dexterity (skill & quickness), wit, and wordplay for it to be successful. Here is an example of the feature "*Everybody and they momma at the car wash this morning.*" Everybody and they momma is signifying that there are an excessive number of people at the car wash that morning.
- *Semantic Inversion*: This feature describes the process whereby Black Language speakers take words and concepts from White Mainstream English lexicon and either reverse their meanings or impose entirely different meanings. Semantic inversion was an act of linguistic empowerment as Africans in America took an alien tongue and made it theirs; simultaneously, they created a communication system that became linguistically unintelligible to the oppressor, even though it was the oppressor's language. One example of semantic inversion is the example from Figure 4.3, which says "*Her outfit is baddd!*" The baddd is an example of semantic inversion because it actually indicates that the dress looks fabulous, which is the opposite of how bad is used in White Mainstream English.
    - Another example of this is with the term *nigga*. Whether we agree or disagree that the term is appropriate, most Black Language-speakers understand that nigga has a variety of meanings and has a different meaning from *nigger*. As Smitherman (1997) points out:

the inversion that has taken place with "nigger" is often misunderstood by people outside of the African American community and is castigated by some African Americans. When used by [Black Language] speakers, nigger has a different pronunciation, spelling, and meaning. In the [Black Language] speech community, the term nigga has a variety of positive meanings. It can mean best friend/your homey, boyfriends/lovers, a really cool associate.

(Smitherman, 1997, p. 19)

- There are negative associations with the term nigga in the Black community as well, but it has a different nuance from the racial epithet nigger.
- After discussing semantic inversion of the term nigga, the students wanted to have more discussion about who gets to use the term, etc. Though this video was unavailable when I worked with the students at LA, I would recommend that teachers who are interested in having critical engagement about the term beyond semantic inversion share a clip[4] by Ta-Nehisi Coates about why certain words don't belong to everyone.

- *Playing the Dozens* (also known as yo momma jokes): There are many ways of engaging in the art of verbal insult. "Playing the dozens" is the most common approach. Playing the dozens is a game—during the game, which is in the call and response format, two opponents make derogatory remarks about each other and each other's family members. Participants usually play the game with someone they know. To stay within the boundaries, they use exaggerated statements that, in reality, may not actually characterize the opponent's family members and family life. The audience judges the opponent's verbal comebacks in determining the actual winner. To discuss the history behind playing the dozens, I showed the students a very brief clip[5] of rapper KRS-One explaining the roots of the feature.
- *Call and Response*: The call and response feature describes the rhythmic exchange between addressers and listeners. The listeners' response during the exchange provides the addresser with cues that the listener is fully engaged in the conversation, which encourages the speaker to continue. One classic example of call and response within the Black speech community occurs at church when the pastor calls out, "can I get an amen?" and the members respond "Amen, Pastor! Hallelujah."
- *Cultural Reference*: The cultural reference feature references cultural items/icons that usually carry symbolic meaning in the Black community. For example, "becky with the good hair."
- *Linguistic Inventiveness | Verbal Creativity*: Verbal inventiveness describes the linguistic improvisation and manipulation of language; the use of language to mark personal style and creativity; the ability to play with and on the word.

Following our discussion about features of Black Language, I had a discussion with the students about how some aspects of Black Language do not translate into White Mainstream English as they communicate unique aspects of the Black experience. To explore these ideas further, I had the students analyze features of Black Language used by Detroit-native hip-hop artist Big Sean during an interview. I specifically selected Big Sean because many of the students viewed him as a hometown hero, and some of his language use was specific to the Detroit community. I asked the students to work in groups and cull features of Black Language from the interview and explain how it reflected Big Sean's theory of reality. Next, I asked the students to translate the interview into White Mainstream English to see if it held the same weight and/or if the message lost its meaning, richness, or flava once translated. The activity about Big Sean's use of language also moved us into a deeper conversation about how Black Language does not get credit for its contributions to the broader English language. I provide a snapshot of this conversation below. In this snapshot, the students, Ms. Helen, and I are discussing the etymology of the word "hoodie."

> "What about hoodie? Is hoodie White Mainstream English?" I asked.
>
> Chase responded, "Yes."
>
> "Okay there is a debate going on," I said to the students. "Some of y'all are saying that the term hoodie is a term that emerged from Black culture ..."
>
> "It is," a few of the students quickly responded.
>
> "But some of y'all are saying hoodie is White Mainstream English," I added. Several of the students responded, "Yesss."
>
> "White people say hoodie. It goes both ways. They be like I got my hoodie on," Allistar pointed out.
>
> "But where did it come from? Have you ever looked at websites or gone into the store looking for what we call hoodie and it being called a what? What was it called? I heard Lola say what it is called," Ms. Helen chimed in from behind her desk.
>
> "A hooded sweater or a hooded shirt?" Janel asked.
>
> "Okay so then we took the term hooded sweater and called it hoodie, and it became so popular that non-Black people are using it now," Ms. Helen explained.
>
> "And this is a very good point right here," I added. "John Rickford, a Black linguist, said that many Black people don't realize that our use of Black words differ from other Americans. And to Ms. Helen's point, a lot of Black vocabulary gets used by White Mainstream English-speakers. Some linguists call this 'crossover.' I think the issue is that white American culture participates in the linguistic and cultural absorption of blackness without any acknowledgement of where it originated from or how Black Language contributes to the broader American English."
>
> "Yep," Ms. Helen added.
>
> "True! Because words in White Mainstream English are usually longer. Like hooded sweatshirt vs. hoodie. I was also thinking that hoodie could also be a play on our use of the word *hood*," Janel explained.

"So basically hoodie might be one of them examples of how we take a term from White Mainstream English and make it our own," I replied.

"I know this language, but I been speaking it all my life. So I cannot tell the difference or did not realize there was so much difference between the two," Chasse commented.

The dialogue between the students, Ms. Helen, and I illustrate why it is necessary for language arts teachers to move beyond simply focusing on the technical differences between Black Language and White Mainstream English. An Antiracist Black Language Pedagogy must include what Jackson (2019) is calling *critically conscious talk* or *CCT*, which is a kind of talk where teachers and students question, interrogate, and dismantle dominant narratives that contribute to Black people's racial suffering.

The final activity the students engaged in for this Black Language Artifact was an activity that asked the students to do an ethnographic analysis of how they use language in their life. Inspired by a unit from Alim's (2007) critical hip-hop language pedagogy, I asked the students to document their communication behavior over the weekend.[6] When the students returned on Monday, many of them shared how surprised they were by how many members of their family actually communicated in Black Language. For instance, Allistar said "At first, I did not think my parents used Black Language, but that's because I thought Black Language was like the slang we use. They [Allistar's parents] don't like that, but they use the real Black Language." Similarly, another student wrote, "Learning how people actually talk and how Black Language isn't just slang showed me that the language is used among different types of people."

Language + Race + Power

Background

It is important to continuously interrogate and exploit the intersections of language, race, and power. Instead of perpetuating linguistic racism in classrooms, language arts teachers should engage their students in critical questioning by asking questions like those included below by Alim and Smitherman (2012), which shows how language is loaded with power.

"Which languages are preferred in which contexts? By whom? Which groups are included—or excluded—by these decisions? Who benefits? … why must Black Americans shift toward styles considered White in order to be 'successful'?" These questions show that the way we talk can either grant or deny us access to social, political, and economic opportunities (think jobs, schools, etc.).

(Alim & Smitherman, 2012, p. 26)

In addition to unpacking these questions, it is important to interrogate the notion of "Standard English." Linguists contend that a standardized language is hypothetical and gets constructed and reconstructed on an ongoing basis by those in positions of power. Lippi-Green (2012) explains that although "non-linguists are quite comfortable with the idea of a standard language ... the term has been variously defined and heavily politicized" (p. 57). Indeed, this notion of Standard English is hypothetical and socially constructed (Lippi-Green, 2012); is maintained through arbitrary ideas that reflect language superiority (Haddix, 2015); is a myth that is used to justify discrimination on the basis of "language markers that signal alliance to certain social groups, primarily those having to do with race, ethnicity, [gender] and economic factors" (Lippi-Green, 2012, p. 15), and it reflects and legitimizes white, male, upper middle-class, mainstream ways of speaking English (Alim & Smitherman, 2012; Lippi-Green, 2012).

Black Language Artifacts 4 & 5: Language, Race, and Power

Black Language Artifacts 4 and 5 were created to get the students at LA to critically interrogate how language, race, and power are interconnected. I started this lesson off by asking students to work in small groups to define "Standard English." This activity was inspired by Lippi-Green's (2012) comment that "non-linguists are quite comfortable with the idea of a standard language, so much so that the average person is very willing to describe and define it, much in the same way that most people could draw a unicorn" (p. 57). My goal for this activity was to get the students to make sense of how an ideology of standardization empowers certain individuals and institutions to make arbitrary decisions about which language is considered standard and impose them on others (Lippi-Green, 2012). The variation in the groups' definitions of Standard English revealed for the students, Ms. Hudson, and I that there were some inconsistencies in our understandings of Standard English and many of our beliefs were not based on linguistic facts. To speak back to some of the myths that arose during group discussions, I read passages from Lippi-Green's (2012) chapter "The Standard Language Myth." Following this discussion, the students engaged in an inquiry-based activity (Figure 4.4) to help them think more deeply about the intersections between language, power, and race.

The activity elicited a variety of responses that illustrated that the students were beginning to challenge language ideologies and problematize the intersections between language, race, and power. For example, Chase said "I feel like if you don't have scientific background on why you have a negative attitude about Black Language, then you shouldn't argue about it just because you feel it's bad and improper." Similarly, Lola added "my concern is that it is not always a bad language because IT IS considered a language." On a follow-up activity,[7] the students continued to problematize the intersections between language, power, and race by examining beliefs that underpin code-switching and language appropriateness. Allistar noted that code-switching and appropriateness approaches empower White

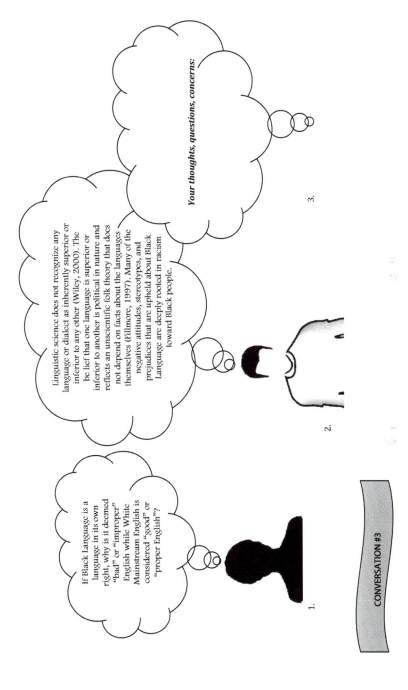

If Black Language is a language in its own right, why is it deemed "bad" or "improper" English while White Mainstream English is considered "good" or "proper English"?

1.

Linguistic science does not recognize any language or dialect as inherently superior or inferior to any other (Wiley, 2000). The be lief that one language is superior or inferior to another is political in nature and reflects an unscientific folk theory that does not depend on facts about the languages themselves (Fillmore, 1997). Many of the negative attitudes, stereotypes, and prejudices that are upheld about Black Language are deeply rooted in racism toward Black people.

2.

Your thoughts, questions, concerns:

3.

CONVERSATION #3

FIGURE 4.4 Conversation About Black Language Worksheet #3

Mainstream English-speakers and disempower Black Language-speakers because these approaches suggest that Black Language should be restricted to informal contexts such as outside, the beach, and the mall whereas White Mainstream English is privileged in nice restaurants, interviews, etc. Allistar goes on to say that these approaches "might make you lose confidence and might make you want to change who you are." Janel responded to the activity by writing:

> Black Language is disempowered by language appropriateness approaches because it's saying you have to be at home or dressed casual to speak Black Language while White Mainstream English is empowered making it seem right to speak in an interview or a church. They're saying White Mainstream English is better than Black Language. This is saying that if your culture is involved with Black Language, then you need to keep it hidden, while if you're speaking White Mainstream English, it is the appropriate culture to show anywhere. This may make a person who speak in Black Language feel bad or that their language is not as good as White Mainstream English.

The second half of this lesson was designed to raise students' awareness of how language, race, and power intersect by exposing them to the ways that Black people have been racially profiled based on the way they speak. I invited the students to the activity by having them participate in an online test that was created by ABC News on *linguistic profiling*. [8] The test[9] (displayed in Figures 4.5 & 4.6) asked the students to listen to a short piece of audio and describe the person's race or ethnicity based on the speech they heard. Once the answer is entered into the answer box, the test reveals the race or ethnicity of the speaker. Before beginning the activity, I asked the students if they think they can determine a person's race or ethnicity based on how they sound. While most of the students pondered on my question, Fetti responded, "sometimes I can with Black people because their voice is a little deeper." Allistar added, "Nine times out of ten, I could identify a person's race based on how they sound."

Following the linguistic profiling quiz, the students viewed four short YouTube video clips to continue to examine the intersections of language, power, and race:

1. A 20/20 special on Black Americans who were denied housing as a result of sounding Black.[10]
2. A public service announcement from HUD (US Department of Housing and Urban Development).[11]
3. A clip of a documentary about the Ann Arbor Black English Case[12] that shows how Black students successfully sued the Ann Arbor schools for linguistic discrimination.[13]
4. A clip of linguist John Baugh describing linguistic profiling.[14]

These YouTube video clips provided the students with more foundation about linguistic profiling in housing and linguistic discrimination in schools and how these

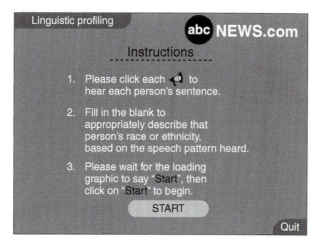

FIGURE 4.5 Linguistic Profiling Quiz #1

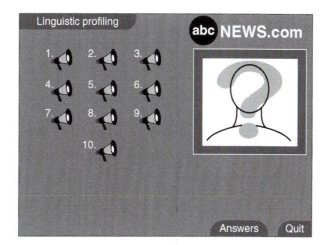

FIGURE 4.6 Linguistic Profiling Quiz #2

instances perpetuate what I am now calling Anti-Black Linguistic Racism. In the section below, I provide a snapshot of how the students responded to the clips.

"Based on what you see in the videos, what might language have to do with race? How is it connected just based on these examples?" I asked.

Lola replied, "So from what I saw in the video about housing, they are able to tell that someone is Black based on the sound of their voice … so they told her [the woman in the video] that the place was no longer available because they could tell that she was Black, and basically they don't want Black people living in that area."

"These clips show that it's not necessarily about the language, but who is speaking the language," Janel said.

"Yeah, all of these videos show that they were discriminated on because of their race," Allistar concluded.

The activities that were included in lesson 4 and 5 speak to Alim's (2007) thinking that by learning about the full scope of their language use and how language can be used against them, students become more conscious of the communicative behavior and the ways "by which they can transform the conditions under which they live" (p. 167).

Beyond Consciousness-Raising: Developing Student Agency & Taking Action

Background

While developing students' linguistic consciousness is crucial to their sense of self and identity, awareness is not enough to bring about social change. An Antiracist Black Language Pedagogy is designed to provide Black students with critical literacies and competencies to name, investigate, and dismantle white linguistic hegemony and Anti-Black Linguistic Racism. Moreover, it is important for students to have an opportunity to create change within their communities. Alim and Smitherman (2012) recommend that language educators motivate youth to:

> engage in community activism around issues of linguistic discrimination. Youth are not only thinking critically about language, but they are also putting their knowledge to work for their communities by developing consciousness-raising campaigns. These campaigns help provide resources for community members for members to engage in the transformation of their neighborhoods.
>
> *(p. 188)*

Unfortunately, my time at LA ended before I could engage the students in community activism. I was, however, able to use this approach in my teacher education courses,[15] which I believe would have been applicable for the students at LA. I provide a brief lesson and recommended activities in the section below.

Black Language Artifact 6: Language, Agency, & Action

This lesson moves the students toward thinking about developing agency, taking a critical stance, and making political choices that support them in employing Black Language for the purposes of various sorts of freedom, including dismantling Anti-Black Linguistic Racism.

Recommended Activities

- Students can create a social media campaign using Facebook, Twitter, Snapchat, Instagram that promotes linguistic justice by exposing Anti-Black Linguistic Racism and Black linguistic appropriation.
- Students can create a public service announcement using YouTube or some other digital tool based on their learning from the Antiracist Black Language Pedagogy.
- Students can facilitate a town hall to discuss the impact of Anti-Black Linguistic Racism on their education, sense of self, and identity.
- Students can write to their school district administration about their language policy if it perpetuates Anti-Black Linguistic Racism and white linguistic hegemony.
- Students can create children's books, graphic novels, zines, etc. that promote linguistic justice for younger children.
- Students can create and facilitate workshops at their schools, community centers, or local libraries that promote awareness of Black Language and Anti-Black Linguistic Racism.
- Students can write letters to their governors and state commissioners of education about linguistic racism and how it is embedded in standardized curricula, test, and language standards.

Language + Solidarity: Examining Linguistic and Racial Violence Across Communities of Color

Background

While it essential for Black students to learn about the roots of their own linguistic background, it is vital that they also develop a critical linguistic awareness of how other communities of color experience racial and linguistic violence and are impacted by linguistic racism. In 2017, Danny Martinez wrote a powerful article that highlights the linguistic violence many Black and Latinx youth face in English classrooms. He argues for a Language of Solidarity Framework across Black and Latinx youth:

> It means working against decades of real divisiveness and opposition that continues to hurt both communities in ways that empower dominant communities. However, providing a language of solidarity for Black and Latinx youth can begin with providing them with real-life examples of solidarity movements that exist in their own communities, locally and nationally. As mentioned previously, countless recent examples can serve as tools to mediate tough conversations. Building on what youth bring to classrooms means that English teachers must be willing to reach into the digital worlds of youth. It means that we have to loosen up on our positions as experts to also learn from students. (p. 192)

I believe that Martinez's framework can be extended to include other communities of color as well. I did not have an opportunity to engage in language solidarity work during my time at LA, but I include recommended activities below to help language and literacy educators imagine what a lesson on language solidarity might look like.

Black Language Artifact 7: Developing a Language of Solidarity

For this artifact, students will develop a critical linguistic awareness and interrogate how other linguistically and racially diverse communities experience racial and linguistic violence and are impacted and are affected by linguistic racism.

Recommended Activities:

- Students can read linguistic narratives by non-Black writers who are impacted by linguistic racism like Amy Tan's (1987) *Mother Tongue* and Gloria Anzaldua's (1987) *How to Tame a Wild Tongue.*
- Students can explore how historically communities of colors have experienced division and opposition that have negatively impacted communities of color as a whole.
- Students can develop an understanding of linguistic and cultural sharing by reading Martinez's (2017) article *Imagining a Language of Solidarity for Black and Latinx Youth in English Language Arts Classrooms,* May's (2019) *Words That Matter: Black and Indigenous Solidarity and the Right to Language,* Paris' (2009) *"They're in My Culture, They Speak the Same Way": African American Language in Multiethnic High Schools.*

"Blacker Than an Essence Fest": A Linguistic Celebration

On the last day of the Black linguistic consciousness-raising component of the Antiracist Black Language Pedagogy, the students, Ms. Helen, and I decided to celebrate Black Language, Black culture, and our once-in-a-lifetime learning experience. We brought in food, Black music, and I brought in the written and YouTube versions[16] of Jamila Lyiscott's poem *Three Ways to Speak English* (see Figure 4.7), a beautiful piece that pays homage to Ebonics and Black Multilingualism. As we watched and read the poem, many of the students shouted and engaged in call and response practices to show that they were feeling Lyiscott's words. Shortly after the video went off, I heard Janel say to Lola, "that was good," and I heard Allistar say, "I'm trilingual." As I looked around the classroom at the Black faces that seemed to be filled with joy, as I listened to them freely communicate with one another in the language that reflected our mother tongue, as I heard their Black voices rap the words to Kendrick Lamar's "Don't Kill My Vibe" in perfect harmony, I could not help but embrace that moment in space and time! This is what Black Linguistic Justice should feel and look like! For a short moment, Anti-Black Linguistic Racism didn't even matter.

Today, a baffled lady observed the shell where my soul dwells
And announced that I'm "articulate"
Which means that when it comes to enunciation and diction
I don't even think of it
'Cause I'm "articulate"
So when my professor asks a question
And my answer is tainted with a connotation of urbanized suggestion
There's no misdirected intention
Pay attention
'Cause I'm "articulate"
So when my father asks, "Wha' kinda ting is dis?"
My "articulate" answer never goes amiss
I say "father, this is the impending problem at hand"
And when I'm on the block I switch it up just because I can
So when my boy says, "What's good with you son?"
I just say, "I jus' fall out wit dem people but I done!"
And sometimes in class
I might pause the intellectual sounding flow to ask
"Yo! Why dese books neva be about my peoples"
Yes, I have decided to treat all three of my languages as equals
Because I'm "articulate"
But who controls articulation?
Because the English language is a multifaceted oration
Subject to indefinite transformation
Now you may think that it is ignorant to speak broken English
But I'm here to tell you that even "articulate" Americans sound foolish to the British
So when my Professor comes on the block and says, "Hello"
I stop him and say "Noooo …
You're being inarticulate … the proper way is to say 'what's good'"
Now you may think that's too hood, that's not cool
But I'm here to tell you that even our language has rules
So when Mommy mocks me and says "ya'll-be-madd-going-to-the-store"
I say "Mommy, no, that sentence is not following the law
Never does the word "madd" go before a present participle
That's simply the principle of this English"
If I had the vocal capacity I would sing this from every mountaintop,
From every suburbia, and every hood
'Cause the only God of language is the one recorded in the Genesis
Of this world saying "it is good"
So I may not always come before you with excellency of speech
But do not judge me by my language and assume
That I'm too ignorant to teach
'Cause I speak three tongues
One for each:

FIGURE 4.7 Jamila Lyiscott's poem

Home, school and friends
I'm a tri-lingual orator
Sometimes I'm consistent with my language now
Then switch it up so I don't bore later
Sometimes I fight back two tongues
While I use the other one in the classroom
And when I mistakenly mix them up
I feel crazy like … I'm cooking in the bathroom
I know that I had to borrow your language because mines was stolen
But you can't expect me to speak your history wholly while mines is broken
These words are spoken
By someone who is simply fed up with the Eurocentric ideals of this season
And the reason I speak a composite version of your language
Is because mines was raped away along with my history
I speak broken English so the profusing gashes can remind us
That our current state is not a mystery
I'm so tired of the negative images that are driving my people mad
So unless you've seen it rob a bank stop calling my hair bad
I'm so sick of this nonsensical racial disparity
So don't call it good unless your hair is known for donating to charity
As much as has been raped away from our people
How can you expect me to treat their imprint on your language
As anything less than equal
Let there be no confusion
Let there be no hesitation
This is not a promotion of ignorance
This is a linguistic celebration
That's why I put "tri-lingual" on my last job application
I can help to diversify your consumer market is all I wanted them to know
And when they call me for the interview I'll be more than happy to show that I can
say:
"What's good"
"Whatagwan"
And of course … "Hello"
Because I'm "articulate"

FIGURE 4.7 (Cont.)

In the next chapter, I include composite counterstories that highlight how the Antiracist Black Language Pedagogy impacted the students at LA. I also offer implications that highlight the importance of Antiracist Black Language Pedagogy in our current historical, political, and racial climate.

Notes

1 https://www.youtube.com/watch?v=EPGx1icFdLQ

2 https://www.pbs.org/video/underground-railroad-william-still-story-coded-spirituals/
3 Rouge Park is a park located in Detroit, Michigan.
4 https://www.youtube.com/watch?v=QO15S3WC9pg
5 https://www.youtube.com/watch?v=Uu-FaOmcSso
6 See appendix A.
7 See appendix B.
8 Linguistic profiling is based on research done by John Baugh that examines perceptual and phonetic studies of linguistic racism.
9 This quiz was available on the University of Iowa's website, but unfortunately it has been removed since the time of the study.
10 https://www.youtube.com/watch?v=3KCL97s1lJg
11 https://www.youtube.com/watch?v=zup2qlFuCDc
12 During the Ann Arbor Black English case, a Federal District Court found the Ann Arbor school district responsible for failing to adequately prepare teachers to respond to the language needs of 11 Black children at the Martin Luther King, Jr. elementary school.
13 https://www.youtube.com/watch?v=KKlmaFQniB0
14 https://www.youtube.com/watch?v=U63FjeeHMoc
15 Example PSA that students in my Spring 2015 ENG 302 course created for their critical language awareness class project: https://youtu.be/r7easj7v2Yk
16 At the time of the study, Lyiscott's TED talk was not available, so we used an older video version of her reciting the poem (http://www.youtube.com/watch?v=Qn_m qVD_7XQ). Here is a link to her current TED talk version of the poem (https://www.ted.com/talks/jamila_lyiscott_3_ways_to_speak_english?language=en)

References

Alim, H. S. (2007). Critical hip-hop language pedagogies: Combat, consciousness, and the cultural politics of communication. *Journal of Language, Identity, and Education*, 6(2), 161–176.

Alim, H. S., & Smitherman, G. (2012). *Articulate while Black: Barack Obama, Language, and Race in the U.S.* Oxford, NY: Oxford University Press.

Anzaldúa, G. (1987). *Borderlands: La frontera*. San Francisco, CA: Aunt Lute.

Baldwin, J. (1979, July 29). If Black English isn't a language, then tell me, what is? *New York Times*. Retrieved September 26, 2008, from www.nytimes.com

Baugh, J. (2015). Use and misuse of speech diagnostics for African American students. *International Multilingual Research Journal*, 9, 291–307.

Gilyard, K. (2005). Foreword. In A. Ball & T. Lardner, *African American Literacies Unleashed: Vernacular English and the Composition Classroom* (pp. xiii–xiv). Carbondale, IL: Southern Illinois University Press.

Green, L. (2002). African American English. In E. Finegan & J. Rickford (Eds), *Language in the USA: Themes for the Twenty-first Century* (pp. 76–91). Cambridge: Cambridge University Press.

Haddix, M. (2015). *Cultivating Racial and Linguistic Diversity in Literacy Teacher Education: Teachers Like Me*. New York, NY, & Urbana, IL: Routledge & National Council of Teachers of English.

hooks, b. (1994) *Teaching to Transgress: Education as the Practice of Freedom*. New York: Routledge.

Jackson, D. (2019) Black symmetry: Carving out a Black space in an eleventh grade classroom. Doctoral Dissertation. Michigan State University. East Lansing, MI.

Lippi-Green, R. (2012). *English with an Accent: Language, Ideology, and Discrimination in the United States.* New York, NY: Routledge.

Lyiscott, J. (2014, February). *Three Ways to Speak English.* [Video file]. Retrieved from: https://www.ted.com/talks/jamila_lyiscott_3_ways_to_speak_english?language=en

Martinez, D. (2017). Imagining a language of solidarity for Black and Latinx youth in English language arts classrooms. *English Education*, 49(2), 179–196.

Mays, K. T. (2019). Words that matter: Black and Indigenous solidarity and the right to language. Retrieved from https://www.beaconbroadside.com/broadside/2019/11/words-that-matter-Black-and-indigenous-solidarity-and-the-right-to-language.html

Paris, D. (2009). They're in my culture, they speak the same way: African American language in multiethnic high schools. *Harvard Educational Review*, 79(3), 428–448.

Rickford, J. R. (2002). How linguists approach the study of language and dialect. Unpublished manuscript, Department of Linguistics, Stanford University, Stanford, California.

Rickford J. R., & Rickford, R. J. (2000). *Spoken Soul: The Story of Black English.* New York, NY: Wiley.

Smitherman, G. (1994). *Black Talk: Words and Phrases from the Hood to the Amen Corner.* New York, NY: Houghton Mifflin.

Smitherman, G. (1997). "The chain remain the same": Communicative practices in the Hip Hop Nation. *Journal of Black Studies*, 28(1), 3–25.

Smitherman, G. (2006). *Word from the Mother: Language and African Americans.* New York, NY: Routledge.

Smitherman, G. (2017). Raciolinguistics, "mis-education," and language arts teaching in the 21st century. *Language Arts Journal of Michigan*, 32(2), 4–12.

Tan, A. (1990). Mother tongue. *The Threepenny Review*, 43, 7–8.

Thomas, V. M. (2018). *Lest We Forget: The Passages from Africa into the Twenty-first Century.* Bellevue, WA: Quarto Publishing Group USA Inc.

Woodson, C. G. (1933). *The Mis-education of the Negro.* Washington, DC: Traffic Output Publication.

5

"BLACK LINGUISTIC CONSCIOUSNESS"

In chapter 3, I shared the students at LA's counterstories to affirm that eradicationist and respectability language pedagogies do not account for the internalized Anti-Black Linguistic Racism, linguistic double consciousness, or the consequences these approaches have on the students' sense of self and identities. Their voices and perspectives underscored the need for alternative language pedagogies that provide students with an alternative way of looking at Black Language and Black identity. In chapter 4, I shared how I responded to this need by describing the Antiracist Black Language Pedagogy that I implemented, and I offered ethnographic snapshots of the students' engagement with it. As you read this chapter, consider the following questions: How are the students at LA impacted by the Antiracist Black Language Pedagogy? How did the Antiracist Black Language Pedagogy develop the students' critical consciousness about Black Language?

Talkin' That Talk: Composite Character Counterstories of the Students' Developing Black Linguistic Consciousness

As noted in chapter 3, before I implemented the Antiracist Black Language Pedagogy, the students' language attitudes and perspectives suggested a complex and nuanced relationship with Black Language that reflected internalized Anti-Black Linguistic Racism or linguistic double consciousness. However, during their engagement with the Antiracist Black Language Pedagogy, I began to observe a shift in their perspectives. I describe this shift as *Black Linguistic Consciousness*, which characterizes how the students are beginning to critically interrogate and consistently resist white linguistic hegemony and Anti-Black Linguistic Racism. Following the consciousness-raising component of the Antiracist Black Language Pedagogy, I invited the students to complete the attitudinal assessment (see Figure 3.1 in chapter 3) once again. I knew that having them complete the activity as a post-attitudinal assessment would give me deep insight about the shifts in their language attitudes, and it would provide the students with an opportunity to reflect on this shift as well. In addition to responding to the language samples and drawing pictures, I asked the students to write a reflection about their growth throughout the curriculum. I present composite character counterstories in the section below which reflect how the students were beginning to develop Black Linguistic Consciousness.

Group Dialogue: Did Your Feelings Change or Remain The Same?

"I want you all to compare your drawings and written responses from today's activity to the drawings and written responses you completed before the curriculum was implemented," Ms. Baker-Bell explained. "Have your feelings about Language A [Black Language] and Language B [White Mainstream English] shifted from before? Did your feelings remain the same? What is the most valuable thing you will take away from this curriculum? Take a few moments to write your responses to these questions in your notebook."

Ten minutes later, Janel raised her hand and shouted, "I'm ready." She continued, "My feelings did change from before because I did not know that slang or Ebonics was even a language or that it had history and roots. The most valuable thing I learned from this study is that the language I use daily is not wrong or incorrect. The language I use is a real language."

"I think when I first started I thought one language was better than the other, but they are both languages people communicate in, and I should not stereotype," Allistar added.

Before he could finish, Fetti Bravo cut him off: "I said the same thang. Your appearance shouldn't portray the way you speak, and I should not judge someone's voice."

Allistar continued, "At first, the image I drew for Language A [Black Language] was a boy sagging and I even took it one step further and called him a thug, but Language B [White Mainstream English] was a well-dressed college student. Now they both are the same because I can speak both languages."

"My attitude changed a little too. I learned that the way I speak is not the wrong way to speak and I can choose when and where not to use it [Black Language]. I always thought the language was wrong. I learned that Black Language is the right way to speak and I am never or was never wrong," Lola replied.

"That's right!" Ms. Baker-Bell nodded at Lola, Allistar, and Janel. "Fetti, you have your hand up. Go ahead!"

"Oh ... I wrote that my feelings did change because I learned that there is a lot of people that actually use Black Language. They are showing who they are. I learned that people that speak Black Language are not ruled out as ghetto. They can be upper class and still speak that way."

"Umm hmm. Umm hmm!" Ms. Baker-Bell replied. "Okay, now I want you all to form smaller groups of about 2–3 individuals. I want you to discuss your drawings and the reflective piece among one another, and then we'll come back together and discuss it as a whole group."

Janel, Lola, & Crystal Collective Composite Counterstory

"What did you draw Janel?" Crystal asked.

"The first image that I drew[1] means I can speak language A [Black Language] wherever I see fit, including in school because language A IS a language [emphasis hers], not slang. Language A should be respected as a knowledge that can be spoken anywhere, and not behind closed doors or in hiding," Janel explains. "My second drawing[2] means that I should be able to speak language B [White Mainstream English] at home without being scrutinized by my family and friends."

"I feel you," Crystal said with excitement. "I was happy to learn about Black Language, but I only use it with my friends. I mostly use White Mainstream English in my home to show respect. It wouldn't seem right talking to my mom or dad in Black Language."

"Wait, your parents don't speak Black Language?" Lola asked.

"I mean, like, they speak it; but, like, they don't really want me to speak it," Crystal responded.

"Umm. Well, Black Language is needed where I'm from. I think it's just about where you're from and where you at and if you know how to relate to them. So if I go somewhere like to the park where other people from my community is at, you talk to them the way they are talking to you," Janel explained.

"I'm frequently in white neighborhoods like Troy, and using White Mainstream English is necessary in these contexts. I wouldn't want people looking down at me a specific way because of the way I talk … 'cause that's embarrassing, and I don't want to be embarrassed in front of family, friends, teachers or anybody," Crystal declared.

"I think it's just however you feel. If you feel like you need to speak White Mainstream English or Black Language, that's your decision. I feel like it shouldn't be based off of how other people feel, though! If you feel like talking like that, you can," Janel maintained as she shrugged her shoulders.

"For me, if I hear somebody judging or saying something about it [Black Language], I might confront them and actually tell them what it's really about and that it's not always a bad thing like people think it is. It's just how they did English [and] how they made those words up. We made our own words so they can't talk about it," Lola insisted.

"I mean I'm not going to be like 'you wrong', but I'm going to know. If a teacher corrects me, I'm gonna be like it's not incorrect. You feel like it's incorrect but it's not incorrect … and I feel like whether it's incorrect to you, it doesn't really matter because this is my mouth," Janel exclaimed.

"You have a smart mouth, Janel!" Lola teased.

Crystal, Lola, and Janel started laughing.

"I mean … that's basically how I been feeling but now I know more about it to back it up," Janel insisted.

"But forreal, my attitude changed so much because I learned some new stuff about Black Language that I did not know. I did not know that it was like, you know, a period where there used to be slaves who put the English language and their language together to make these words. I did not know that. It made me feel like we weren't dumb because if they were making up a new language, we made something too. I mean we're not dumb like most people think we are," Lola emphasized.

"Yesss! My thinking improved from just learning it was an actual language in the first place," Janel sighed. "The first time I did this assignment, I drew a picture of me for both language samples. The one with Black Language, I was with my friends ... and in the one with White Mainstream English, I drew a picture of me in front of the teachers after I switched it up. But this time, my pictures show that I can use Black Language in school and at home."

"My drawing show that you can't talk about somebody else language because that's how they learned at a young age. My representation A is showing a girl and her friend talking in Black Language. Representation B is showing a girl saying don't use Black Language, use White Mainstream English," Lola explained.

"Why is the girl saying don't use it?" Janel questioned.

"Because there's always going to be ignorant people who think you shouldn't," Lola responded.

Reflecting on Janel's & Lola's Black Linguistic Consciousness

In the composite character counterstory, we are able to observe a shift in Janel's and Lola's thinking around Black Language. From chapter 3, we learned that Janel was feeling conflicted and ambivalent toward Black Language before engaging the Antiracist Black Language Pedagogy. That is, she embraced Black Language and felt compelled to defend its honor, yet there were moments where she acquiesced to politics of respectability and perpetuated Anti-Black Linguistic Racism. Lola often made comments that reflected internalized Anti-Black Linguistic Racism. We do not see this ambivalence and internalized Anti-Black Linguistic Racism reflected in the counterstory involving Janel and Lola. Instead, we are able to see how Lola and Janel's engagement with the Antiracist Black Language Pedagogy provided them with the tools to challenge and interrogate white linguistic hegemony and Anti-Black Linguistic Racism. For example, when Crystal states that she will continue to communicate in White Mainstream English because she does not want anyone to look down on her, Janel explains that she should not have to make decisions about language based on someone else's opinion. This example illustrates that Janel now recognizes that attitudes about language are not based on linguistic facts about the language themselves but more so reflect anti-Black racism toward the speaker.

Both Lola and Janel indicated that their perspectives toward Black Language changed following their involvement with the Antiracist Black Language Pedagogy. Lola explains that her attitude changed after learning that enslaved Africans developed Black

Language, and Janel indicated that her attitude improved after learning about the linguistic and rhetorical features of Black Language. The historical and linguistic background of Black Language are usually omitted in a traditional language education, but as Janel and Lola point out, these vital aspects were instrumental in them developing Black Linguistic Consciousness. However, as Crystal's character reveal, there were a few students who were still struggling with linguistic double consciousness. That is, Crystal was feeling conflicted about fully embracing Black Language because she understands that she still has to navigate and negotiate her language in spaces that will continue to uphold white linguistic hegemony. This is a real concern and illustrates that an Antiracist Black Language Pedagogy alone cannot solve Anti-Black Linguistic Racism and white linguistic hegemony. We must continue to think about how we can work toward changing the structures, systems, and institutions that perpetuate linguistic racism and language subordination.

Allistar & Fetti Collective Composite Counterstory

"Let me see what you drew, bro." Fetti chuckled as he reached out for Allistar's drawing.

"Nah, man! You got jokes," Allistar laughed.

"Man, let me see this," Fetti said as he snatched Allistar's drawing off of his desk. "Why you draw a picture of the same dude twice?" (see figure 5.1)

"I drew the same boy for both languages because he is like me. He integrate both languages wherever he at. It is a part of me. It has become one of my traits as a human being just like my culture and religion," Allistar replied

"That's what's up! Because in the beginning you was saying that people who talk like that are thugs," Fetti reminded Allistar.

"Fa sho! I did not know we spoke like that. I thought it was a bad term and ghetto. But she [Baker-Bell] changed it and now I think of it as heritage and culture … and it's a good language to use. I think the language should be preserved because it helped us form African American culture," Allistar exclaimed.

Fetti nodded in agreement.

"At first, I thought Black Language was like the slang we use. I did not know about the real Black Language … like the structure and stuff. When I started thinking more about it, I realized that if I wasn't using Black Language, I wouldn't be able to communicate with some of the people around me. Some people, that's the only language they know mainly. So it would like cut me off from them. If you can't understand each other, you can't really speak," Allistar clarified.

"And it would make you, like, be a little behind at school because if you don't get something from the teacher and a kid wants to help you … the kid won't talk like the teacher, he'll talk in Black Language," Fetti explained.

"Real Talk," Allistar responded.

"How are y'all doing in this group? Don't forget to discuss any of the activities that contributed to any shifts in your thinking!" Ms. Baker-Bell said to Fetti and Allistar before walking toward the next group.

"Oh yeah. For me, the activity that she had us do where we guessed the people's race based on their voice helped my thinking," Fetti responded.

FIGURE 5.1 Allistar's Drawing for Post–Attitudinal Assessment

"For me, it was the little sheet of paper she gave us with the features and how to use it. It was kind of like a dictionary," Allistar recalled. "Oh, and the girl[3] from the video who said she said she was trilingual. 'Cause she said she speaks at church, home, and with her friends. And that's how I thought of that drawing because I use the same languages as she did. So I could speak a different way at home, church, and at school. So I'm trilingual," Allistar declared.

Fetti replied, "Yeah her poem was cold! What other language you speak?"

"Trinidad. It's like a Caribbean language. I can't explain it. It's really my dad's language. He used to have like a real Caribbean voice but now it's like a little bit more English but you still hear that he's from somewhere else," Allistar said.

"This makes me want to do more research about my culture, you know?" Fetti murmured.

"Me too! And I have to say … I learned that you shouldn't be judged just because you speak a certain way. Because you say your words different, you shouldn't be criticized. There are more things you could be criticized about, but never language."

Reflecting on Allistar's and Fetti's Black Linguistic Consciousness:

As Fetti points out, Allistar's attitude and perspective before the Antiracist Black Language Pedagogy suggested that he internalized white linguistic hegemony and perpetuated anti-Blackness and Anti-Black Linguistic Racism. This was reflected in the way he described Black Language speakers as intellectually and morally inferior. I observed a shift in Allistar's thinking throughout the Antiracist Black Language Pedagogy that illuminated how he was beginning to develop Black Linguistic Consciousness. For instance, Allistar explains that he initially thought that Black Language was simply slang and a bad way of communicating, but he now realizes that Black Language reflects his heritage and culture. Allistar and Fetti both noted specific aspects of the Antiracist Black Language Pedagogy that shifted their thinking. Though Fetti was challenging Anti-Black Linguistic Racism before I implemented the consciousness-raising component of the Antiracist Black Language Pedagogy, he indicated that the linguistic profiling activity and quiz shifted his thinking. Allistar explained that his attitude toward Black Language shifted after he learned about the features of Black Language and viewed Lyiscott's poem, *Three Ways to Speak English*. Allistar and Fetti's counterstory also brought attention to their cultural connection to Black Language and the significance of it in their communities. Allistar explained that Black Language connects him to the people around him (family, friends, neighbors, etc.), and without it, he would lose that connection with those who love him and share the same theory of reality.

Black Linguistic Justice: A Way Forward

Smitherman (2006) reminds us that the study of Black Language could open up avenues of self-exploration and discovery. The students at LA counterstories speak for themselves! The Antiracist Black Language Pedagogy provided Janel, Allistar, Lola, and Fetti with:

- a language to name their unique experiences with linguistic racism
- critical capacities to question and interrogate linguistic oppression
- African American epistemologies that allow them to view Black Language, literacy, and identity in complex and sophisticated ways
- space to critically reflect and interrupt their own internalized Anti-Black Linguistic Racism, and most importantly
- a language education that affirms and values their racial and linguistic backgrounds and experiences, which is invaluable for their sense of self and identity.

As I reflect on my time at LA, there are many things I wish I could have done. I often return to Janel, Allistar, Lola, and Fetti's wisdom. I like to wrap my brain around their words and ponder on what they were telling me then that I could not receive during the time that the study took place. I credit these linguistic geniuses for helping me give birth to a pedagogical innovation that will surely benefit so many Black Language speakers like themselves.

Linguistic Justice: Black Language, Literacy, Identity, and Pedagogy is designed to give Black students the tools to liberate themselves from oppression. However, let me also point out that the Antiracist Black Language Pedagogy that I outline in this book offers ALL students and their teachers a critical linguistic awareness of Black Language and windows into broader conversations about anti-Blackness, language and identity, language and power, language and history, linguistic racism, and white linguistic and cultural hegemony. These critical capacities are just as important—if not more important—for white students as they are for Black students and other students of color, as white students are more likely to perpetuate Anti-Black Linguistic Racism and uphold white linguistic hegemony by way of their privilege, power, and lack of awareness of language varieties other than their own. And although an antiracist Black Language education and pedagogy are specific to the linguistic and racial needs of Black students, the principles and pedagogy can be adjusted and applied to benefit other language groups.

Like anything else, language and literacy educators cannot implement an Antiracist Black Language Pedagogy without interrogating their own Anti-Black Linguistic Racism or internalized Anti-Black Linguistic Racism. Language and literacy educators have to be honest with themselves about the ways they uphold and perpetuate white linguistic hegemony in their classrooms and in their everyday lives. You can't be out here saying that you believe in linguistic diversity at the same time of shutting students down as soon as they open their mouths. You have to be about this life for real for real! You have to be ready and willing to challenge everything you once understood about language and what students need in a language education. You have to be ready for the messiness that comes with this process. You also don't have to do everything by yourself—I encourage language and literacy educators to position themselves as learners and allow your students to do their part by teaching you. TRUST … they already know so much about linguistic and racial injustice. Alim and Smitherman (2012) call for language educators and scholars to continue to think about the "linguistic dimensions of race—in order to move the national conversation on race forward" (p. 169). This is what I hope I contributed to with this book, but I invite you to join me on the frontlines of the language wars. Let's transform our language education and create something we ain't never seen before!

In closing, I leave you with the words of Toni Morrison about Black people's love of Black Language.

> The language, only the language … It is the thing that Black people love so much—the saying of words, holding them on the tongue, experimenting with them, playing with them. It's a love, a passion. Its function is like a preacher's: to make you stand up out of your seat, make you lose yourself and hear yourself. The worst of all possible things that could happen would be to lose that language.
>
> *(qtd. in Alim & Smitherman, 2012)*

Notes

1 See Figure 3.4. in chapter 3.
2 See appendix C.
3 Lyiscott, J. [TEDSalon NY2014] (2014, February). *Three Ways to Speak English.* [Video file]. Retrieved from: https://www.ted.com/talks/jamila_lyiscott_3_ways_to_speak_english?language=en

References

Alim, H. S., & Smitherman, G. (2012). *Articulate while Black: Barack Obama, Language, and Race in the U.S.* Oxford, NY: Oxford University Press.

Smitherman, G. (2006). *Word from the Mother: Language and African Americans.* New York, NY: Routledge.

6

"THUG LIFE"

Bonus Chapter: Five Years After Leadership Academy

The following is a passage from Angie Thomas' award-winning young adult novel *The Hate U Give* (2017).

> That means flipping the switch in my brain so I'm Williamson Starr. Williamson Starr doesn't use slang—if a rapper would say it, she doesn't say it, even if her white friends do. Slang makes them cool. Slang makes her "hood." Williamson Starr holds her tongue when people piss her off so nobody will think she's the "angry black girl." Williamson Starr is approachable. No stank-eyes, none of that. Williamson Starr is non-confrontational. Basically, Williamson Starr doesn't give anyone a reason to call her ghetto. I can't stand myself for doing but I do it anyway.
>
> —*Starr, from the novel* The Hate U Give

In the passage, the protagonist Starr, a Black teenager who attends a predominantly white high school (Williamson) but lives in a predominantly Black community (Garden Heights), is describing how she navigates and negotiates her Black identity in a white space that expects her to perform whiteness, especially through her language use. Albeit fictional, Thomas' depiction of Starr accurately captures the cultural conflict, labor, and exhaustion that many Black Language-speakers endure when code-switching; that is, many Black Language-speakers are continuously monitoring and policing their linguistic expressions and working through the linguistic double consciousness they experience as a result of having to alienate their cultural ways of being and knowing, their community, and their blackness in favor of a white middle class identity. African American young adult literature like *The Hate U*

Give provides Black youth with an opportunity to see their racial and linguistic realities reflected in literature.

Since my work with the students at Leadership Academy in 2013, I have been thinking a lot about the power of African American young adult literature within an Antiracist Black Language Pedagogical Framework. Charity Hudley and Mallinson (2014) posit that "by examining literature, students gain an appreciation for the rich diversity of language, and they are exposed to a medium through which authors and readers can grapple with critical social issues" (p. 73). Yet, whenever I ask my preservice students how Black Language structures were addressed when they read African American literature like Zora Neale Hurston's *Their Eyes Were Watching God*, Alice Walker's *The Color Purple*, Lorraine Hansberry's *A Raisin in the Sun*, and *Fences* by August Wilson, many of them reveal that they did not discuss language at all. This is unsettling as literature "often tells the stories of regular people, living their lives, and speaking in their varied tongues" (Charity Hudley & Mallinson, 2014, p. 73), and it provides a rich opportunity for students in English Language Arts (ELA) classrooms to examine how language and race inform identity and experience. Indeed, there is no venue more capable of discussing, critiquing, and dismantling linguistic and racial injustice than literary studies and the ELA classroom (Borsheim-Black & Sarigianides, 2019; Charity Hudley & Mallinson, 2014; Sealey-Ruiz, 2016). Over the last few years, there has been a surplus in young adult African American novels that work to dismantle Anti-Black Linguistic Racism and provide an outlet to conscientize students to the historical, cultural, political, linguistic, and racial underpinnings of Black Language. In addition to *The Hate U Give*, novels like *I Am Alphonso Jones* by Tony Medina and *Dear Martin* by Nic Stone provide a rich foundation for literacy educators to put our current racial and linguistic realities in conversation with the critical analytical tools we offer in ELA classrooms.

In this bonus chapter, I offer Black Language Artifacts that are inspired by work I did with my preservice English education students[1] in a course that I designed and named *Linguistic (IN)Justice: A Black Counterstory of the English Language*. I began using *The Hate U Give* (hereafter *THUG*) as my primary young adult literature text in the course for a few reasons: (1) it provides my students with a rich foundation to explore how identity is conceived through language expression, (2) it engages students in a language study that goes beyond White Mainstream English, (3) it is contemporary representation of how Black Language reflects Black people's ways of knowing, interpreting, surviving, and being in the world, and (4) the book shows how it is nearly impossible to separate a person's language from their racial positioning in society (Flores & Rosa, 2015). Additionally, the novel provided important opportunities to explore the intersections of language, race, racial violence, Anti-Black Linguistic Racism, and power. In the second half of this chapter, I highlight a series of teacher-scholar-activist events, aptly named *THUG* Event Series, that I organized and involved my students in based on *THUG*. I close out this chapter by including an interview from one of my students about her experience participating in my course and in the *THUG* Event Series.

Linguistic Justice As a Framework in English Teacher Education Courses

In the section that follows, I offer seven Black Language Artifacts that demonstrate how I am using the Antiracist Black Language Pedagogy as a framework to prepare preservice English Education students to use literature to work against Anti-Black Linguistic Racism. Each Black Language Pedagogy artifact listed below contains three sections that lay out important information about each artifact in relation to *THUG*: (1) a *description* that explains the theme, (2) a list of potential *activities* that can be used to engage the students in the theme, and (3) *supplemental resources* that can be read or viewed to provide students with foundational information about the theme. The artifacts build off of one another but do not necessarily have to be followed in any particular. The Black Language Artifacts that follow are not intended to be a prescriptive approach to an Antiracist Black Language Pedagogy; instead, these are ideas that can implemented, altered, or used for inspiration to help teachers think through how to use literature in the pursuit of linguistic and racial justice.

Black Language Artifact 1: Black Language and Identity

Description

For this artifact, students examine the intersection of language, culture, and identity within the Black community.

Activities

- Have students explore the linguistic identity of the characters in *THUG* by performing a linguistic analysis. Have the students examine how, when, and where Starr uses language.
- Have the students examine how Black Language reflected the character's ways of knowing, interpreting, and surviving in the world.
- Have the students examine the relationship between Black Language and Black culture in the novel.
- Have the students examine the tension Starr experienced with language and race throughout the novel.
- Have the students write a linguistic memoir that examines their racial and linguistic identities. For example, students might consider writing about how

language is used within their families and communities; their experiences with linguistic racism; etc.

Supplementary Resources

- Have the students read or view the following texts that represent language, culture, and identity within the Black community.

  - *From Ghetto Lady to Critical Linguist* by Geneva Smitherman (1990).
  - *Reclaiming My Language: The (Mis)education of Wonderful* by Wonderful Faison (2014).
  - *Three ways to speak English* by Jamila Lyiscott (2014).

Black Language Artifact 2: Language, History, and Culture

Description

For this artifact, students participate in a language study that examines the historical, cultural, and political underpinnings of Black Language.

Activities

- Have students examine the difference between a pidgin and a creole.
- Have students examine dialectologists and creolists' perspectives on the history and development of Black Language.
- Have students explore the influence of language planning during enslavement.
- Have students learn about the history and translate coded spirituals.
- Have students explore the ways in which enslaved Africans and their descendants were denied access to literacy by law.
- Have students explore the history of Black Language in relation to the issues related to language and power that surfaces in *THUG*.

Supplementary Resources

- Have the students read or view the following texts that provide windows into the historical, cultural, and political underpinnings of Black Language:

  - A PBS clip about the underground railroad and coded spirituals.[2]
  - A short clip from "Do You Speak American" about linguistic profiling, the origin of Black Language and Gullah.[3]
  - The article "Use and misuse speech diagnostics for African American students" by John Baugh (2015).

Black Language Artifact 3: The Study of Black Language

Description

For this artifact, students participate in a language study that examines the structural and discourse features of Black Language.

Activities

- Have students examine sociolinguists' perspectives about the standard language ideology.
- Have students explore Black grammatical structures (syntax, semantics, phonology, etc.) represented in *THUG*.
- Have students explore Black discourse/rhetorical features represented in *THUG* (signifyin', semantic inversion, call & response, etc.).
- Have students conduct a rhetorical analysis to investigate Angie Thomas's choices for using Black Language at various moments and with various characters throughout the novel.
- Have students do a mini-ethnographic study of how language is used within their own linguistic communities.

Supplementary Resources

- Have the students read the excerpts from the following texts that examine the structural and discourse features of Black Language:
    - *The Standard Language Myth*, a chapter from the book *English with an Accent* by Lippi-Green (2012).
    - *Spoken Soul: The Story of Black English* by Rickford & Rickford (2000).
    - *Signifying, narrativizing, and repetition: Radical approaches to theorizing African American Language* by Williams-Farrier (2016).
    - *Change the Game*, a chapter from the book *Articulate While Black* by Alim & Smitherman (2012).

Black Language Artifact 4: Language & Power

Description

For this artifact, students examine the intersection of language and power.

Activities

- Have students examine who decides whose language gets to be considered academic language, standard, official, normal, appropriate, etc.

- Have students examine systems that perpetuate linguistic oppression (linguistic hegemony, standard language ideology, etc.)
- Have students examine the relationship between language and power in *THUG*.
- Have students interrogate the concept of code-switching through Starr's experiences in *THUG*. Have the students unpack the tension Star experiences when code-switching at Williamson.
- Have students investigate how language has been used to profile and discriminate against Black Language-speakers.

Black Language Artifact 5: Language & Racial Positioning

Description

For this artifact, students examine the intersections between language and race. They also have opportunities to investigate the relationship between language and anti-blackness as one way of understanding Anti-Black Linguistic Racism.

Activities

- Have students examine the presence of white linguistic hegemony in *THUG* and how Starr navigated and negotiated it.
- Have students examine the definition of Anti-Black Linguistic Racism and investigate how its presence was reflected in *THUG*.
- Have students examine how Anti-Black Linguistic Racism is perpetuated through systems of power (schools, housing, law, etc.).
- Have students examine their own experiences with Anti-Black Linguistic Racism and white linguistic hegemony.
- Have students examine how Black Language is culturally appropriated, co-opted, and commodified by white mainstream culture.

Supplemental Resources

- Have the students do the following to examine the relationship between language and racism:
  - Read *I Can Switch my Language, but I Can't Switch My Skin: What Teachers Must Understand About Linguistic Racism* by Baker-Bell (2017).
  - Watch a clip about linguistic profiling an ABC News.[4]
  - Explore Anti-Black Linguistic Racism within our court systems by examining how Rachel Jeantel's, witness in the George Zimmerman trial, testimony was treated for her use of Black Language.[5]

Black Language Artifact 6: Language, Agency, and Action

Description

For this artifact, students develop agency, take a critical stance, and make political choices that support them in employing Black Language for the purposes of various sorts of freedom, including dismantling Anti-Black Linguistic Racism.

Activities

- Have students perform a rhetorical analysis of how Black writers and speakers have used BL powerfully for various sorts of freedom (creative writers/speakers, academic writers/speakers, activists, etc.).
- Have students explore and practice using Black Language powerfully and rhetorically.
- Have students organize teach-ins, create PSAs, write books, etc., that promote critical consciousness of BL and Anti-Black Linguistic Racism.
- Have students create language policies that protect and preserve Black Language and Black Language-speakers within their communities, schools, and the world.

Supplementary Resources

- Have the students read the following texts to aid them in developing linguistic agency, taking critical stances, and making political choices that will support them in employing Black Language for the purposes of various sorts of freedom, including dismantling Anti-Black Linguistic Racism:
  - StayWoke: *The language and literacies of #BlackLivesMatter movement* by Richardson and Ragland (2018).
  - Conference on College Composition and Communication (1974) *Students' Right to Their Own Language* resolution.

Black Language Artifact 7: Black Language & Music & Memes

Description

I created the following activity to have students perform a critical linguistic analysis on lyrics and /or memes. I describe the activity in two steps below.

Activity

Step 1: Using the lyrics/ memes you were given, answer the following:

- Interpret the meaning embedded in this piece (break down the hidden meanings represented).
- What is largely being signified in and through this piece?
- How does Black Language play a role in this piece?

  a   What features of Black Rhetoric are reflected in and through this example?

- How does this example "disturb the peace" (Smitherman, 1997)?

  a   How does it resist dominant culture?

  b   How does it push back against Black oppression/ White Supremacy?

Step 2: Present findings to the class.

- Provide a summary/ interpretation of the piece based on your findings.
- Provide specific examples of how Black Language was represented in this piece.

I've used this activity to deconstruct the lyrics to *Black Effect* by the Carters,[6] *Changes* by Tupac Shakur,[7] and *Don't Touch My Hair* by Solange.[8] I have also used the video version of *This is America* by Childish Gambino.[9]

Black Language Artifact 8: Developing a Language of Solidarity

Description

For this Black Language Artifact, students develop a critical linguistic awareness and interrogate how other linguistically and racially diverse communities experience racial and linguistic violence and are impacted and are affected by linguistic racism.

Activities

- Read linguistic narratives by non-Black writers who are impacted by linguistic racism.
- Learn how historically communities of colors have experienced division and opposition that have negatively impacted communities of color as a whole.
- Develop an understanding of linguistic and cultural sharing.

Supplementary Resources

- Have the students read the following texts to help them develop a broader understanding of linguistic racism, linguistic violence, and how white linguistic and cultural hegemony negatively impacts communities of color.

    a   "Imagining a language of solidarity for Black and Latinx youth in ELA classrooms" by Danny Martinez (2017).

    b   "'They're in my culture, they speak the same way': African American language in multiethnic high schools" by Django Paris (2009).

    c   "Mother tongue" by Amy Tan (1990).

    d   "How to tame a wild tongue" by Gloria Anzaldua (1987).

    e   "Words that matter: Black and Indigenous solidarity and the right to language" by Kyle T. Mays (2019).

Linguistic Justice as Community and Teacher-Scholar-Activism

I organized the *THUG* Event Series, from November 2018 to January 2019. The event series was designed around both the book and film adaptation of *THUG*, and it provided my English Education students and our surrounding communities with an opportunity to engage in topics around anti-blackness, racial violence, police brutality, and linguistic racism. The series included four events:

- *THUG Film Viewing*: I organized a trip for students in my English Education course to view the film adaptation of *The Hate U Give*.
- *THUG Dialogue*: The *THUG* dialogue was a campus-wide discussion about the film adaptation of the book and its relationship to our current racial realities. The dialogue also provided participants with a rich opportunity to complicate film adaptations of books.
- *THUG Collaborative*: For this event, I organized a collaborative between students in our English Education courses and a high school ELA class in Detroit, Michigan to support the implementation and facilitation of *The Hate U Give*, and provide MSU English Ed students with authentic experiences teaching and learning alongside linguistically and racially diverse students.
- *THUG Teach-In:* The teach-in/work-in was a professional development event for educators interested in receiving support and resources for teaching about race and racism in the literacy classroom using the book, *The Hate U Give*. The teach-in included a variety of teaching demonstrations, presentations, and discussions facilitated by MSU English Ed faculty and secondary ELA teachers from various schools throughout Michigan.

I include Black Language Artifacts from some of the events in the section below.

THUG Film Viewing & THUG Dialogue

My English education students were required to read *THUG* before our trip to see the film. Two weeks after the film, I organized a dialogue and live Twitter chat at MSU. The following questions and topics (also represented in Appendix D) guided our dialogue.

1. Before getting into our critical questions, let's DISCUSS what the book and film captured well. What do the book and film allow us to accomplish?

2. *On Character Omissions …*

    ● DeVante and Starr's grandmother were dynamic characters who had important roles in the book, yet they were left out of the film. How did these omissions impact the film?

3. *On Chris …*

    ● In the film, Chris, Starr's white boyfriend, tells her he does not see color. This scene is not reflected in the book. What might have been the purpose of including this scene in the film? Why are comments like "I don't see color" problematic?

    ● In the book, Chris joins Starr, Seven, and DeVante at the protest. This scene is left out of the film. What are your thoughts about this?

    ● Some reviewers have deemed the section of the book where Starr tells Chris he will not understand her situation because he is white an example of reverse racism. Reverse racism doesn't exist; however, this comment creates space for us to have a discussion about why it doesn't.

    ● What does Chris' character suggest for white people in general, and white allies in particular?

4. *On Colorism …*

    ● The cover of *The Hate U Give* book featured Starr as dark skinned and many have suggested that she was described as dark skinned in the book. Yet, Amandla Stenberg, a biracial actress, plays Starr in the film. Some reviewers have suggested that this mismatch sheds light on the media's bias views regarding light skinned or mixed women, who they consider to be more presentable, more attractive, or more accepted. Indeed, the inclusion of dark skinned actors in Hollywood movies has been very minimal and fickle. What are your thoughts?

5. *On Different Messages…*

    ● Some have suggested that the book and the film offer two separate critiques. For example, the book ends with Starr connecting Khalil's death, at the hands of a white police officer (#115), to the murders of actual Black people who were killed by police and vigilantes. Starr specifically states on page 443:

    > It would be easy to quit if it was just about me, Khalil, that night, and the cop. It's about way more than that though, It's about Seven. Sekani. Kenya. Devante. It's also about Oscar. Aiyana.

Trayvon. Rekia. Michael. Eric. Tamir. John. Ezell. Sandra. Freddie. Alton. Philando. It's even about that little boy in 1955 who nobody recognized at first—Emmett."

Some viewers have suggested that this represented how the book challenges a policing system that kills Black people. On the other hand, the film ends with a shocking twist, in which Starr's younger brother, Sekani, pulls out a gun on King, the neighborhood drug dealer. This scene coupled with Starr's message that "we have the power to break this cycle" have some viewers feeling as if the film makes Black people primarily responsible for their own oppression by not asking its audience to challenge the police system, but instead, focus on "Black-on-Black crime." What are your thoughts?

6. *On white screenwriters…*

- The screenwriter of *The Hate U Give*, Audrey Wells, was a white woman. What role might this have played in the way in which the film was presented and the way the story was told? What gets lost when white screenwriters write screenplays that are based on Black experiences?

7. *On THUG and BlackLivesMatter …*

- Some have touted *The Hate U Give* film as the first Black Lives Matter movie. However, many, including #BlackLivesMatter co-founder, Patrisse Cullors, have stated that *THUG* film is not a #BLM film; it is the antithesis. What are your thoughts about this statement in relation to BLM's mission?

8. *On THUG & Tupac's theory of THUG LIFE …*

- Tupac's theory of THUG LIFE, which was an acronym for **T**he **H**ate **U G**ive **L**ittle **I**nfants **F**ucks **E**veryone, was "a critique of a White-supremacist-capitalist system that treats Black and poor children with contempt, depriving them of resources, and ultimately causing the whole society to suffer the consequences." Angie Thomas stated that Tupac's theory influenced *The Hate U Give*. Was Tupac's critique adequately captured in the book? What about the film?
- Do you agree with Angie Thomas that the scene with Sekani pulling the gun on King was a visual of Tupac's Thug Life?

9. *On THUG & Black Language …*

Smitherman (2006) describes Black Language as

a style of speaking English words with Black Flava—with Africanized semantic, grammatical, pronunciation, and rhetorical patterns. [Black Language] comes out of the experience of U.S. slave descendants. This shared experience has resulted in common language practices in the Black community. The roots of African American speech lie in the counter language, the resistance discourse, that was created as a communication system unintelligible to speakers of the dominant master class.

(Smitherman, 2006, p. 3)

- How did *The Hate U Give* book and film help us make sense of how Black Language reflects Black people's ways of knowing, interpreting, surviving, being, and resisting in the world?
- How does Starr problematize the notion of code-switching?

THUG Collaborative

For this project, I organized a collaborative between my pre-service English Education students and a Detroit high school teacher and her students. The purpose of the collaborative was to support the classroom teacher in the implementation and facilitation of THUG, and provide my students with authentic experiences teaching and learning alongside high school students. The collaborative involved my students developing curricular materials focused on using THUG to work toward linguistic justice and presenting those materials in the form of a teaching demonstration to the high school students and their teacher. The students and their teacher in turn provided my preservice students with feedback about how they experienced the curricular materials, and they offered feedback and ideas for how the preservice teachers could continue this work in their future classrooms.

To facilitate the collaborative, I secured funds from MSU and to purchase the teacher and her students a classroom set of books, movie passes, and transportation to see the film, and funds to host a field trip for the students and their teacher to visit at MSU and participate in the teaching demonstration. One of my former high school students paid the expenses for the students' transportation to and from campus as a way of paying it forward. To prepare for the collaboration, the teacher and her students read the book and saw the film separately from my students and me. However, the classroom teacher asked me to create a mini-workshop that connected Tupac's theory of THUG LIFE with the themes represented in the novel, which provided me an opportunity to interact with the high school students before they met with my preservice students.

THUG Teach-in

As noted above, the THUG teach-in was a professional development event that I organized for educators interested in receiving support and resources for teaching about race and racism in the literacy classroom using literature. The teach-in brought together teachers from all across the state of Michigan. I intentionally selected two English teachers from Flint, Michigan; one English teacher from Detroit, two graduate students from Michigan State University, and a poet from New York (originally from

Detroit) to facilitate sessions for the teach-in. The facilitators shared teaching demonstrations that illustrated how English teachers can use *THUG* in the pursuit of racial justice. During this session, the facilitators engaged participants in a concentrated and serious dialogue that illuminated how *THUG* can be a resource that supports teachers to: (1) work toward racial and intersectional justice in their classrooms and communities, (2) learn about activities they can engage in with lessons that make visible the set of curricular and pedagogical implications *THUG* has for classroom praxis, and (3) explore critical and creative approaches and activist tools that teachers can implement in their classrooms when teaching THUG. Below, I provide a brief, but more detailed description of the facilitators' teaching demonstrations.

- *Demonstration 1*: The facilitator[10] illustrated how educators can use the "Jam Session" technique to have small, intimate discussions within their classroom to develop an environment where teachers and students can share their feelings on the complex themes found in *THUG*. This activity can be used at the beginning of a unit and allows students to discuss and be inspired by Angie Thomas's musical inspiration, Tupac Shakur, with the examination of his song *Changes*.
- *Demonstration 2*: The facilitator[11] demonstrated how teachers can use *THUG* to inspire student research, make writing culturally relevant for an authentic audience, and create a succinct culminating project that all readers can benefit from. In particular, this facilitator shared some of the work her students engaged in while reading *THUG*, including a research based lesson and student projects that were displayed during National Black Lives Matter in Schools week.
- *Demonstration 3*: The facilitator[12] used the main character, Starr, in *THUG* to explore politics of respectability in the age of Cardi B and Tiffany Haddish as it impacts young Black girls. Participants in this session learned about how to introduce these topics in their own classrooms by participating in a mini close reading and a literature circle. The facilitator provided the participants with resources that will help them use *THUG* to address race, racism, gender, and sexuality in their classrooms.

How Black Language and Black Literature Can Inspire Activism: Concluding Thoughts from a Future English Educator[13]

A few months after the course ended, my student, Tiffany Whittington, was interviewed and featured on our university's website regarding her experiences in my course and her involvement with the THUG events. With Tiffany's permission, I include the interview, *How a Book Can Inspire Activism,* in the section below.

Tiffany's interview

Tiffany Whittington is a junior pursuing a degree in English and a minor in TESOL (Teaching English as a Second Language) in the College of Arts and Letters. She plans to use her education, literature, and language to influence and change the lives of others, while finding ways to be an activist and give back to her community.

> Activism has grown to be important to me over the years … especially when it directly relates to my community. When I was presented the chance to make even just the slightest difference, I jumped at it.
>
> It was the beginning of the semester for me in Dr. April Baker-Bell's English 302 course. I didn't really know what to expect, but I knew that we would be reading Angie Thomas's novel *The Hate U Give*, so I was thrilled to see what that was about.
>
> Once I began the book, I realized that it focuses on very serious issues that happen in the Black community ranging from police brutality and oppression, to drugs and gang violence. It is an amazing book; once I started it, my eyes were glued to the pages.
>
> One of the reasons I think the book is so good is because it did more than just tell the issues of a Black community. It was uplifting and even acted as a sense of empowerment. It showed how one individual could use her voice to stand up against the odds and fight towards a change in society.
>
> The book was so outstanding, when Dr. Baker-Bell informed us that the English department would be hosting an event series based off of *The Hate U Give*, I knew that I wanted to participate as much as I could. The events consisted of a trip to see the book's film, a dialogue and Twitter chat, a collaborative with Detroit Denby High School and, lastly, a teach-in for educators and prospective educators.
>
> I attended every event. The movie wasn't as great as the book, but the weakness in the film provoked interesting conversation during the dialogue and Twitter chat. I got to see many different perspectives of issues relating to the book, coming from students, professors and even members of the community.
>
> The final two events—the collaborative and teach-in—were my favorite. I especially enjoyed becoming an activist as I considered how to approach the events presented in *THUG* through the eyes of an educator.
>
> The collaborative with the high school consisted of my peers and I creating and teaching lesson plans to be used in conjunction with teaching the book *The Hate U Give*. Through this experience, I was able to use my voice and teach high school students things that I wish I would've known when I was their age.
>
> The teach-in was a similar experience, as educators from various backgrounds presented their own unique lesson plans that they created to accompany the book. Both experiences challenged me to consider how I'll teach sensitive topics like racism and police brutality when I am a future educator. However, after seeing others do it, I know that it is completely possible, and even more important in order to create an inclusive classroom environment and inspire future activists.

Notes

1 The racial makeup of the students who take my course each semester is representative of a majority-white teaching force. In the course that I describe throughout this chapter, my students included one Black woman, 11 white women, and two white men, a troubling demographic that is also reflective of the undergraduate English education program at MSU. When teaching this course to the majority of white

students, it is important for me to get them to "acknowledge their own racial identity, to name the ways that racism works, and to apply new understandings to the world around them" (Borsheim-Black & Sarigianides, 2019, p. 4) as part of the self-work they have to engage in and work through in order to embrace an Antiracist Black Language Pedagogical framework.

2 [Public Broadcasting Service] (2012, February 5). Coded Spirituals. [Video file]. Retrieved from: https://www.pbs.org/video/underground-railroad-william-still-story-coded-spirituals/

3 [Kmm0010] (2008, April 27). Linguistic profiling. African American English origin, Gullah. [Video file]. Retrieved from https://www.youtube.com/watch?v=EPGx1icFdLQ

4 Linguistic Profiling/ Subordination: https://www.youtube.com/watch?v=rwoLpS9dDhs

5 https://stateofopportunity.michiganradio.org/post/do-we-judge-people-way-they-speak

6 *Black Effect,* The Carters: https://www.youtube.com/watch?v=3HVqowAv_YQ#action=share

7 *Changes,* Tupac Shakur: https://youtu.be/9G6ro-c0C5E

8 *Don't Touch my Hair,* Solange: https://youtu.be/YTtrnDbOQAU

9 *This is America,* Childish Gambino: https://music.youtube.com/watch?v=VYOjWnS4cMY&feature=share

10 The facilitator was Jessyca Matthews.

11 The facilitator was Carrie Mattern.

12 The facilitator was Silver Danielle.

13 Neither my Linguistic (In)Justice English Education course nor the *THUG* event series was intended to be a research project, so I do not have any transcribed responses from the high school students or the teacher about their experiences with the *THUG* collaborative. However, I was able to refer to my preservice teachers' comments on my teaching evaluations regarding how they experienced the course and the *THUG* collaborative. I include those below:

- I really loved Dr. Baker-Bell as a professor, and I feel I learned So MUCH in this course. I think that my favorite part was the teaching demonstration with the high school students because we got to apply what we learned.
- I think the course is incredibly effective in the way it makes not only more-informed teachers but human beings. Class was made all the more engaging by Dr. Baker-Bell, who was so passionate about the course content, it was hard not to feel the same way.
- I had no understanding of linguistic oppression before this course, but now that I know about it. I cannot imagine not addressing this in a classroom. I feel so much more prepared to talk about linguistic oppression and the ties between language and culture.
- I learned that Black Language is a language and will not assume people who speak it are uneducated.
- This course exposed me to different perspectives in a more in-depth way than ever before, drawing me further into an understanding of racial issues than I could have before experienced. It also drew me into a more profound appreciation of linguistics and the unique stories that language tells, which has greatly inspired both me and my writing.

References

Alim, H. S., & Smitherman, G. (2012). *Articulate while Black: Barack Obama, language, and race in the U.S.* Oxford, NY: Oxford University Press.

Anzaldúa, G. (1987). *Borderlands: La frontera.* San Francisco, CA: Aunt Lute.

Baker-Bell, A. (2017). I can switch my language, but I can't switch my skin: What teachers must understand about linguistic racism. In E.MooreJr., A. Michael, & M. W. Penick-Parks (Eds.), *The Guide for White Women Who Teach Black Boys* (pp. 97–107). Thousand Oaks, CA: Corwin Press.

Baugh, J. (2015). Use and misuse of speech diagnostics for African American students. *International Multilingual Research Journal*, 9, 291–307.

Borsheim-Black, C., & Sarigianides, T. S. (2019). *Letting Go of Literary Whiteness: Antiracist Literature Instruction for White Students.* New York, NY: Teachers College Press.

Charity Hudley, M., & Mallinson, C. (2014). *We Do Language. English Language Variation in the Secondary English Classroom.* New York, NY: Teachers College Press.

Conference on College Composition and Communication (CCCC). (1974). Students' right to their own language position statement. Retrieved from http://www.ncte.org/library/NCTEFiles/Groups/CCCC/NewSRTOL.pdf

Faison, W. (2014, October 16). Reclaiming my language: The (mis)education of wonderful. [Blog post]. Retrieved from http://www.digitalrhetoriccollaborative.org/author/moarhai420/

Flores, N., & Rosa, J. (2015). Undoing appropriateness: Raciolinguistic ideologies and language diversity in education. *Harvard Educational Review*, 85(2), 149–171.

Lippi-Green, R. (2012). *English with an Accent: Language, Ideology, and Discrimination in the United States.* New York, NY: Routledge.

Lyiscott, J. (2014, February). *Three Ways to Speak English.* [Video file]. Retrieved from: https://www.ted.com/talks/jamila_lyiscott_3_ways_to_speak_english?language=en

Martinez, D. (2017). Imagining a language of solidarity for Black and Latinx youth in English language arts classrooms. *English Education*, 49(2), 179–196.

Mays, K. T. (2019). Words that matter: Black and Indigenous solidarity and the right to language. Retrieved from https://www.beaconbroadside.com/broadside/2019/11/words-that-matter-Black-and-indigenous-solidarity-and-the-right-to-language.html

Paris, D. (2009). They're in my culture, they speak the same way: African American language in multiethnic high schools. *Harvard Educational Review*, 79(3), 428–448.

Richardson, E., & Ragland, A. (2018). #StayWoke: The language and literacies of #BlackLivesMatter Movement. *Community Literacy Journal*, 12, 27–56.

Rickford J. R., & Rickford, R. J. (2000). *Spoken Soul: The Story of Black English.* New York, NY: Wiley.

Sealey-Ruiz, Y. (2016). Why Black girls' literacies matter: New literacies for a new era. *English Education*, 48(4), 290–298.

Smitherman, G. (1997). "The chain remain the same": Communicative practices in the Hip Hop Nation. *Journal of Black Studies*, 28(1), 3–25.

Smitherman, G. (1990). *Talkin That Talk: Language, Culture, and Education in African America.* New York, NY: Routledge.

Smitherman, G. (2006). *Word From the Mother: Language and African Americans.* New York, NY: Routledge.

Tan, A. (1990). Mother tongue. *The Threepenny Review*, 43, 7–8.

Thomas, A. (2017). *The Hate U Give.* New York, NY: Balzer & Bray.

Williams-Farrier, B. (2016). Signifying, narrativizing, and repetition: Radical approaches to theorizing African American language. *Meridians*, 15, 218–242.

LANGUAGE IN YOUR EVERYDAY LIFE

How do you use Black Language in your everyday life? For this activity, you are being asked to collect and analyze your actual lived experiences for two days to uncover how you use Black Language in your everyday life. More specifically, I want you to document your use of Black Language, i.e., the features you are using, the context(s) you are using it in, and whom you are using it with. Please record your findings on the chart below. Begin collecting your language use today, and return this sheet by Monday.

Features: What did I say?	Setting: Where was I when I said it?	Participants: Who did I use the language with?	Other Notes

LANGUAGE, IDENTITY, POWER, AND CULTURE ACTIVITY

Speakers of Black Language are often told to code-switch (use Black Language in "informal" contexts and White Mainstream English in "formal" contexts) to avoid the "consequences" that may occur from using Black Language. For this activity, I want you to examine the following recommendations about appropriate settings to use Black Language and White Mainstream English through the lenses of (identity, power, and culture).

Informal Places/Black Language	Formal Places/White Mainstream English
• baseball field	• nice restaurant
• the beach	• wedding
• home on the weekend	• awards ceremony
• church	• church
• outside	• museum
• mall	• interview
• farm	

Informal Clothes/Black Language	Formal Clothes/White Mainstream English
• jeans and sweatshirt	• suit and tie
• bathing suit	• nursing uniforms
• sports uniforms	• military uniforms

Please write your initial thoughts, questions, or concerns about the above recommendations:

Language and Power

Which language is empowered and which language is disempowered by the above recommendations? Explain.

Language and Culture

If Black Language is deemed appropriate only in informal settings and White Mainstream English is deemed appropriate only in formal settings, what might these recommendations imply about the cultures that speak Black Language? White Mainstream English? Explain.

Language and Identity

How might the above recommendations about language impact the identity formation or self-esteem of a person who communicates in Black Language? Explain.

JANEL'S SECOND DRAWING

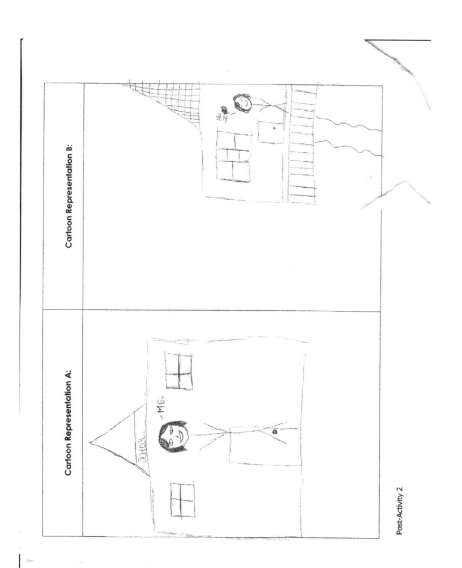

THUG DIALOGUE QUESTIONS

"Absolutely riveting!"
—JASON REYNOLDS, bestselling coauthor of *All American Boys*

THE
HATE
U
GIVE

ANGIE THOMAS

1. Before getting into our critical questions, let's DISCUSS what the book and film captured well. What do the book and film allow us to accomplish?

2. *On Character Omissions …*

- DeVante and Starr's grandmother were dynamic characters who had important roles in the book, yet they were left out of the film. How did these omissions impact the film?

3. *On Chris …*

- In the film, Chris, Starr's white boyfriend, tells her he does not see color. This scene is not reflected in the book. What might have been the purpose of including this scene in the film? Why are comments like "I don't see color" problematic?
- In the book, Chris joins Starr, Seven, and DeVante at the protest. This scene is left out of the film. What are your thoughts about this?
- Some reviewers have deemed the section of the book where Starr tells Chris he will not understand her situation because he is white an example of reverse racism. Reverse racism doesn't exist; however, this comment creates space for us to have a discussion about why it doesn't.
- What does Chris' character suggest for white people in general, and white allies in particular?

4. *On Colorism …*

- The cover of 'The Hate U Give' book featured Starr as dark skinned and many have suggested that she was described as dark skinned in the book. Yet, Amandla Stenberg, a biracial actress, plays Starr in the film. Some reviewers have suggested that this mismatch sheds light on the media's bias views regarding light skinned or mixed women, who they consider to be more presentable, more attractive, or more accepted. Indeed, the inclusion of dark skinned actors in Hollywood movies has been very minimal and fickle. What are your thoughts?

5. *On Different Messages …*

- Some have suggested that the book and the film offer two separate critiques. For example, the book ends with Starr connecting Khalil's death, at the hands of a white police officer (#115), to the murders of actual Black people who were killed by police and vigilantes. Starr specifically states on page 443:

  > It would be easy to quit if it was just about me, Khalil, that night, and the cop. It's about way more than that though, It's about Seven. Sekani. Kenya. Devante. It's also about Oscar. Aiyana. Trayvon. Rekia. Michael. Eric. Tamir. John. Ezell. Sandra. Freddie. Alton. Philando. It's even about that little boy in 1955 who nobody recognized at first—Emmett.

Some viewers have suggested that this represented how the book challenges a policing system that kills Black people. On the other hand, the film ends with a shocking twist, in which Starr's younger brother, Sekani, pulls out a gun on King, the neighborhood drug dealer. This scene coupled with Starr's message that "we have the power to break this cycle" have some viewers feeling as if the film makes Black people primarily responsible for their own oppression by not asking its audience to challenge the police system, but instead, focus on "Black-on-Black crime." What are your thoughts?

6. *On white screenwriters …*

- The screenwriter of *The Hate U Give*, Audrey Wells, was a white woman. What role might this have played in the way in which the film was presented and the way the story was told? What gets lost when white screenwriters write screenplays that are based on Black experiences?

7. *On THUG and BlackLivesMatter …*

- Some have touted *The Hate U Give* film as the first Black Lives Matter movie. However, many, including #BlackLivesMatter co-founder, Patrisse Cullors, have stated that THUG film is not a #BLM film; it is the antithesis. What are your thoughts about this statement in relation to BLM' mission?

8. *On THUG & Tupac's theory of THUG LIFE …*

- Tupac's theory of THUG LIFE, which was an acronym for **T**he **H**ate **U G**ive **L**ittle **I**nfants **F**ucks **E**veryone, was "a critique of a White-supremacist-capitalist system that treats Black and poor children with contempt, depriving them of resources, and ultimately causing the whole society to suffer the consequences." Angie Thomas stated that Tupac's theory influenced *The Hate U Give*. Was Tupac's critique adequately captured in the book? What about the film?
- Do you agree with Angie Thomas that the scene with Sekani pulling the gun on King was a visual of Tupac's Thug Life?

9. *On THUG & Black Language …*

Smitherman (2006) describes Black Language as

a style of speaking English words with Black Flava—with Africanized semantic, grammatical, pronunciation, and rhetorical patterns. [Black Language] comes out of the experience of U.S. slave descendants. This shared experience has resulted in common language practices in the Black community. The roots of African American speech lie in the counter language, the resistance discourse, that was created as a communication system unintelligible to speakers of the dominant master class.

(Smitherman, 2006, p. 3)

- How did *The Hate U Give* book and film help us make sense of how Black Language reflects Black people's ways of knowing, interpreting, surviving, being, and resisting in the world?
- How does Starr problematize the notion of code-switching?

References

Smitherman, G. (2006). *Word From the Mother: Language and African Americans*. New York, NY: Routledge.

INDEX

Page numbers in *italics* refer to figures, those in **bold** indicate tables.